Food
Design and Culture

Laurence King Publishing
in association with Glasgow 1999

Published 1999 by Laurence King
Publishing, London
in association with Glasgow 1999
Festival Company Ltd
Laurence King Publishing is an
imprint of Calmann & King Ltd
71 Great Russell Street
London WC1B 3BN
Tel: +44 171 831 6351
Fax: +44 171 831 8356
e-mail: enquiries@calmann-king.co.uk
www.laurence-king.com

Copyright © 1999 Glasgow 1999
Festival Company Ltd
78 Queen Street
Glasgow G1 3DN
Tel: +44 141 287 7346
Fax: +44 141 248 8754
info@glasgow1999.co.uk

A catalogue record for this book is
available from the British Library.

ISBN 1 85669 163 2

Designed by Stephen Coates, August
Design assistance: Julia Morlock
and Jean Garrett
Picture research by Suzanne Hodgart

Printed in Italy

Glasgōw 1999
UK City of
Architecture
and Dēsign

Food   Design and Culture

Edited by
Claire Catterall

*With essays by
Stephen Bayley,
Paola Antonelli,
Joanna Blythman,
Jonathan Glancey,
Will Alsop,
Ettore Sottsass and
photographic essay
by Martin Parr*

Contents

Contributors

Will Alsop is an architect and Professor of Architecture at the Vienna Technical University. He is a Fellow of the Royal Society of Arts and the Royal Institute of British Architects, and a member of the Architectural Institutes in Germany and Russia. He has lectured in architecture at numerous universities throughout the world. His clients include Toyota, Reuters and the BBC. He was shortlisted for the Stirling Prize in 1997. He has participated in numerous solo and group exhibitions, most recently *Alsop Paintings & Architecture* at the Architekturgalerie, Stuttgart (1998).

Paola Antonelli has a Master's Degree in Architecture from the Polytechnic of Milan and has worked as an architecture and design critic and curator. She joined the Museum of Modern Art, New York, in 1994, as a curator in the Department of Architecture and Design. For MoMA she organized the exhibitions *Mutant Materials in Contemporary Design* (1995), *Thresholds: Contemporary Design from the Netherlands* (1996), *Achille Castiglioni: Design!* (1997) and *Projects 66: Campana/Ingo Maurer* (1998).

Stephen Bayley is a well-known commentator on design, style and popular culture. He has been a design consultant on projects for numerous companies, including Mercedes-Benz, TAG-Heuer, Chrysler, Fiat and United Distillers. He appears frequently on radio and television and has lectured throughout the world. In 1989 he was made a *Chevalier de l'Ordre des Arts et des Lettres*, France's top artistic honour. In 1995 he was the Periodical Publisher's Association Columnist of the Year. His books include *The Conran Directory of Design* (1985), *Commerce and Culture* (1989) and *Taste* (1991).

Joanna Blythman is one of the UK's leading investigative food journalists. She writes for *The Guardian* regularly and contributes to several other publications and broadcasts on food issues. She has won three prestigious Glenfiddich awards for her writing, a Caroline Walker Media Award and a Guild of Food Writers Award. She is the author of the award-winning *The Food We Eat* (1996) and *The Food Our Children Eat* (1999).

Claire Catterall is a curator, writer and commentator on historical and contemporary design and visual culture. Recent projects as an independent curator include *Design of the Times* at the Royal College of Art, and *Powerhouse::UK* for the Department of Trade and Industry. Current projects include the exhibitions *Stealing Beauty: British design now* at the Institute of Contemporary Arts, London, and *Food: Design and Culture* for Glasgow 1999 City of Architecture and Design.

Jonathan Glancey is the Architecture and Design correspondent of *The Guardian*. From 1989 to 1997 he was a regular contributor to *The Independent*. He also works on radio and television. His books include *New British Architecture* (1988) and *The New Moderns* (1990). He is an Honorary Fellow of the Royal Institute of British Architects.

Martin Parr is a photographer and member of the Magnum Agency. His work has been exhibited all over the world in both group and solo shows. His prints appear in the collections of many museums, including San Francisco Museum of Modern Art; Museum for Fotokunst, Denmark; Bibliothèque Nationale, Paris; Sprengel Museum, Hanover; and Tokyo Metropolitan Museum of Modern Art. He is also the author of several books, including *Signs of the Times* (1992) and *Small World* (1995).

Ettore Sottsass graduated as an architect from Turin Polytechnic in 1939, and opened an office in Milan in 1946. Since 1958 he has been a design consultant for Olivetti but is also active in fields as various as ceramics, jewellery, decorations, lithographs and drawing. He has taught and exhibited widely. In 1980 he established Sottsass Associati with other architects, and in 1981 founded Memphis. He has received the Compasso d'Oro on many occasions, and has lectured and exhibited all over the world.

Previous pages: As the twentieth century progresses, so the food on our shelves is less a product of nature than a product of technology and design. These are just some of the processed foods made by the Kraft company.

Television and magazines help to fuel the aspirational quality of food. Opposite: Philip Harben (1953), among the first of a new breed of television cooks who brought professional standards of culinary skills into the homes of thousands of people. Right: While food products are increasingly designed to take the toil out of cooking, manufacturers rely on conjuring up images of authentic home cooking to gain popular appeal.

Following pages: Details of supermarket trolleys, baskets, a refrigerator and a till receipt.

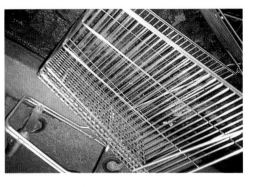

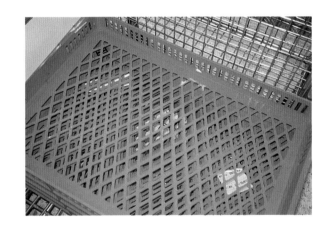

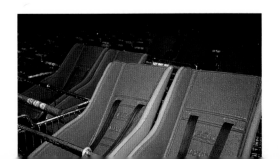

```
        SAINSBURY'S SUPERMARKETS LTD
              FINCHLEY ROAD
        TELEPHONE NO. 0171 4331493


                                    £
        BAKED BEANS                0.28
        FRUIT COCKTAIL             0.19
        * HAPPY COLA               0.10
  *PICK & MIX
   0.06 lb @ £2.48/lb             0.15
  *PICK & MIX
   0.06 lb @ £2.48/lb             0.15
        PASTA CASARECCE            0.52
        SUP/NOODLES CHNS           0.49
        BARBIE PASTA               0.39
        POP TARTS 300G             1.25
        TOMATO KETCHUP             0.55
        GRN GIANT NIBLET           0.49
        GINGER PRESERVE            0.49

        12 ITEMS PURCHASED
        BALANCE DUE                5.05

  CASH                             5.10
  CHANGE                           0.05

     REWARD QUALIFYING BAL         5.05


     DATE: 07 JAN 99   TIME: 20:32
     LOC: 030 OP:  141 TRANS: 1941


     TO COLLECT SAINSBURY'S POINTS
     REGISTER FOR A REWARD CARD
              TODAY

       UP TO DOUBLE YOUR MONEY
        WITH SAINSBURY'S REWARD
     VOUCHERS. SEE IN STORE LEAFLET.
```

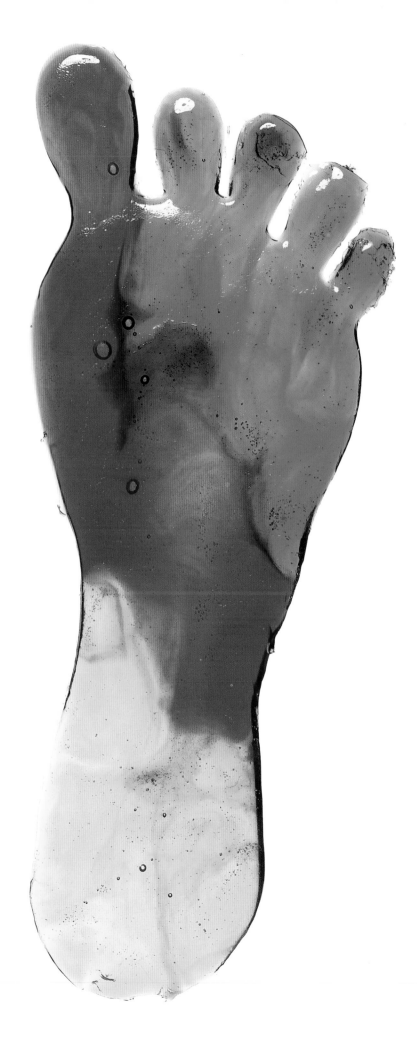

Previous pages: McDonald's, Beijing, China was the largest hamburger restaurant on the planet when it opened in 1995.

'Snackitecture' Opposite, top row, l–r: Major League Grand Slams. Limited-edition puffed corn cereal launched in the US in Spring 1998 by General Mills; Mysterious Peanut. Sold in sweet shops around the world, the chewy peanut has the texture of a stale marshmallow and the taste of pure sugar. The ingredients and manufacturer are elusive; Heinz Barbie Pasta Shapes in tomato sauce. Currently available only in the UK. Shapes include a necklace, bow, high-heeled shoes and heart. Second row, l–r: Lucky Charms Frosted Wholegrain Oat Cereal with Marshmallows. First appeared in 1964; Macaroni & Cheese Dinner (Bugs Bunny and Friends). One million boxes of Kraft Macaroni and Cheese are sold every day in the US; Swiss Cheese Baked Snack Cracker. Nabisco owns nearly 55 per cent of the $2.6 billion cracker market, with the help of the best-selling cracker in the US, the Ritz. Third row, l–r: Trolli Mini Burger has a fruity flavour and an aerated, foamy consistency; Marshmallow Alpha-Bits, the 1957 cereal made in the US by Post. Shown here is the expressionistic rendering of a yo-yo; Candy Stamper. Once licked it doubles as an ink stamp.

Bottom row: Smiley Goldfish Cracker. Pepperidge Farm's salty goldfish gained a limited-edition grin after a whimsical suggestion from the company president. The beatific smile emerged after several experiments with dough and dye and some rejected 'smirking' fish, and helped increase sales by 30 per cent; Big Choice Bubble Gum Cigars. Introduced in the early 1950s by a Philadelphia chewing gum company that also makes 'mouthwash', a sweet that turns the chewer's mouth various vivid colours.

Left: Mega Foot Gummi. The lickable gelatin-based foot was created at Beacon Sweets and designed so that individual toes could be removed from the mould without them tearing off. Below: Candy Blox. Sweets shaped like plastic toys and made out of pressed dextrose, adapting the technology used to manufacture pills.

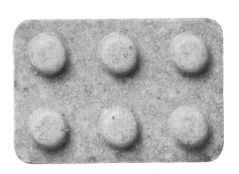

Opposite: Shaped Jelly Dessert. Jell-O was first sold in 1897 by a cough medicine maker, and is based on an 1845 recipe for a sugary dessert made with gelatin. Over a million packets a day are now eaten.

This page, top row, l–r: Striped, rainbow-shaped biscuit; Sugar-coated, coloured sweets; second row l-r: Kaboom Toasted Oat Cereal. Introduced by General Mills in 1969 as a 'breakfast food' and consisting of 43.8 per cent sugar; Trix Wildberry Corn Puffs. A new addition to the General Mills classic of 1954, this piece suggests a genetically engineered rasp-blueberry. Air-puffed cereals like Trix were first produced in 1937.

Below: Gummi Watch. Originally known as the 'Roll-lix' (roll it around the wrist and lick it), the Gummi Watch was forced to change its name shortly after its introduction in 1966 in response to pressure from Rolex, the watch company. Bottom row, l–r: Bubble cards. Two-colour playing cards, made with a sheet-fed printing press filled with food-grade ink colouring; Candy Cigarettes. The cigarette-like sweet made by World Candies of Brooklyn, New York, with sugar, guar gum and beef gelatin; Marpo Marshmallow Fun Cones. Started in 1936, the company now makes up to 23 million cones a year.

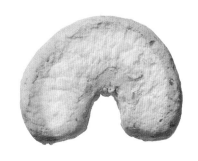

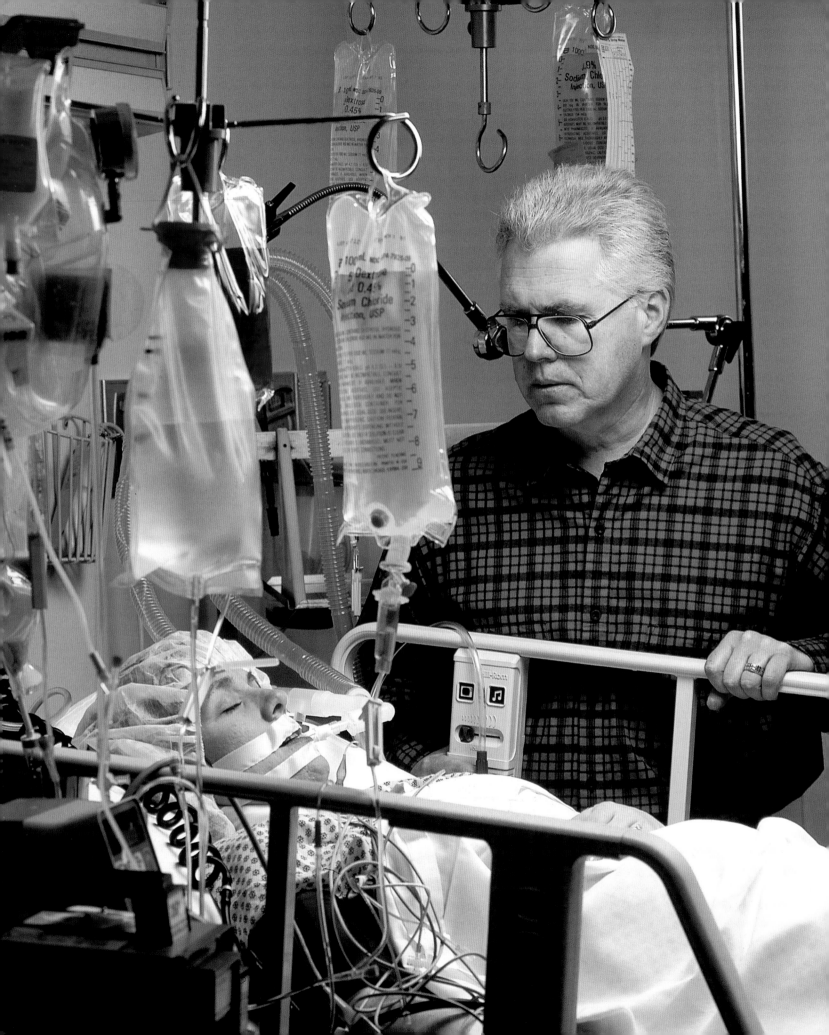

Opposite: Artificial feeding by intravenous drip – a tube inserted via the nasopharynx to the oesophagus is attached to a bag of nutrients. This provides all the nourishment required to keep a human being alive when unable to feed.

Below: Fresh organic produce from the award-winning Merricks Organic Farm, Somerset.

Food: a design for the senses

Claire Catterall

The Last Supper (detail) Leonardo da Vinci, 1495–97. Throughout history food has been associated with ritual. At the Last Supper Christ identified himself with bread, a staple food in the Holy Land. Following his instructions to 'do this in remembrance of me' Christians still eat bread – or, in more recent times, a wafer – in a symbolic partaking of their Saviour's body.

There are few things as important to us as food. Like oxygen, it is the very stuff of life. Yet what we eat means so much more to us than mere sustenance. It represents our humanity, it defines us. Indeed, our relationship with food is one of the fundamental things that separates us from animals. What we eat describes who and what we are, and how we should like to be. It tells of our society, the culture and age we live in; it speaks of politics, economics and geography. It encompasses love, friendship, family; marks ritual, celebration, solace; articulates hopes, dreams and aspirations. The history of food shows us the history of mankind itself. In the words of the celebrated French gastronome and bon viveur Jean Anthelme Brillat-Savarin (1755–1826): 'The pleasures of the table are of all times and all ages, of every country and of every day; they go hand in hand with all our other pleasures, outlast them, and in the end console us for their loss.'

Food makes its transformation from mere fuel to something meaningful through the careful combination of tastes, textures, odours, colours and shapes. While it may be overstating the case to say that cooks are designers of food, there are distinct parallels between cooking and design. As Stephen Bayley points out in his book *Taste* (1991): 'Because cooking involves the conception and execution of an idea, the assembling of functional components into a pleasing whole ... this makes it similar to design.' And just as the products we design are more than tools created in response to certain physical needs, so food is required to do so much more than simply fill our bellies. In the same way that we design products for comfort, aesthetic pleasure and emotional fulfilment, so we apply design to food not just in response to our physical hunger, but also to feed our senses.

But as more and more food products appear on our supermarket shelves, so the intersection of food and design becomes ever more blurred. Today, food is a mass-produced consumer commodity, and as such has as much claim to be a designed object as the Ford motor car. Ready meals, for example, go through much the same process of development as new industrial products. And there are countless other food products – from breakfast cereals to children's sweets, pre-packaged sandwiches to cooking sauces – that require the same research, development, engineering and marketing skills as does the latest Nintendo game. The insatiable desire for the new, improved and innovative applies equally to food as to toys, cars and domestic appliances. In 1995 there were 4,596 new food and drink products introduced on to the British market alone – the equivalent of 88 a week.

In the US, the ultimate concept in ready meals has already been brought on to the market by a company called Zesto Therm. It is an 'ambient' meal packed with its own self-contained heating unit containing salt and magnesium alloy. When water is added the resulting solution breaks down the alloy, producing sufficient heat to warm the food in 15 minutes. Each package contains the food, a heater tray, a pouch of water for activating the heater, salt, pepper, utensils and a napkin: an astonishing feat of design and engineering technology, not to mention careful market research. Whether or not it achieves commercial success remains to be seen. The increasingly rapid pace of technological and scientific change in the late

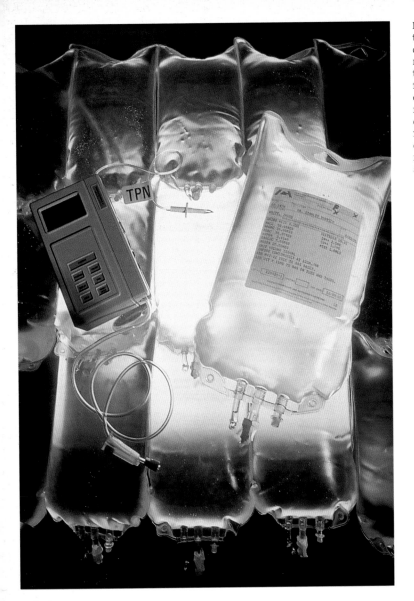

twentieth century means that, as we approach the next millennium, there are even more opportunities for the paths of design and food to cross. Special foods need to be developed for our modern times – foods for space travel, low-calorie food and meal-replacement liquid diets, high-performance foods for athletes, McDonald's burgers that are uniform in all the 79 countries in which they are sold, intravenous drips. Airline meals have to be designed to withstand extremes of temperature and combat the effects of high altitude on the palate – not to mention fitting like a jigsaw puzzle on a small plastic tray together with utensils and condiments. In the last ten years technology has impacted on the scope of food in ways never before imaginable – we now face the prospect of the genetic make-up of food itself being engineered to suit our requirements.

Apart from the design of food products themselves, the design practitioner's skills are evident in every other aspect of our relationship with food, from the supermarkets we buy our food from, to the packaging the food is wrapped in; from the kitchens, dining rooms and restaurants in which we cook and eat, to the tools – appliances, kitchen utensils, crockery, cutlery – we cook and eat with. This close connection between food and the environments in which we act out our relationship with it hints at the increasingly important role food plays in our lives today, and points to yet another area where food and design enjoy a close bond, that is in how we choose to describe and define ourselves.

Recent years have seen an unprecedented growth of interest in food. Cookery shows proliferate on our television screens, chefs are becoming as famous as pop stars, cookbooks outsell the latest 'sex and shopping' blockbusters, subscriptions to the plethora of new 'gastroporn' magazines are spiralling, and no Sunday supplement is complete without its celebrity restaurant reviewer. Today, dining out is an everyday occupation rather than a special treat, while restaurants and recipes alike are becoming increasingly international, reflecting a remarkable cross-fertilization of cultures, tastes and ingredients. Not only is the culture of food itself becoming increasingly sophisticated, the design of the environments in which we cook and eat, as well as the tools we cook and eat with, share equal billing in the public's current obsession. Designer kitchens and kitchen appliances, restaurants kitted out to reflect the latest look – be it school refectory, dentist's clinic or Pre-Raphaelite boudoir – all take up at least as many column inches in the Sunday supplements as does food. Why are we suddenly so fascinated by food and the culture of food? At a time

Left and opposite: Oz refrigerator and Teo oven prototype (below), two of Zanussi's latest products for the style-conscious consumer, introduce alternatives to the traditional 'white boxes' characteristic of most kitchen appliance design. Both were designed by Roberto Pezzetta. Appliance design now takes its lead from a host of diverse influences, from the car industry to the fashion catwalk as much as from changes in lifestyle. The design of the Oz refrigerator has a softer, more curvilinear form, reflecting a change from the hard-edged designs of the 1980s.

when the very structure of society is undergoing radical transformation, does our current obsession act as symptom or panacea for our times?

The breakdown of the traditional family unit and the increasing number of people living on their own suggests that we might be gradually losing sight of the traditional culture of cooking and eating. The Rennie 'Eating into the Millennium' report (1997) found that nearly half the people in the UK now eat their evening meal while sitting on the sofa watching television, with over a third of people tucking into more take-aways than they were five years ago. In Britain alone, approximately one million pounds a day is spent on chilled pre-cooked dinners and meals for one, a growth of 24 per cent from the 1970s to the 1990s and the most dynamic sector in the UK grocery market. As the cycle of food production, supply, distribution and consumption becomes increasingly governed by technology, with the prospects of genetically modified food and shopping on the internet becoming a reality, so the traditional notions associated with food are being ever more eroded. But it is ironic that at a time when the traditional role played by food in our culture and society is disappearing, we are becoming nations of obsessive gourmands.

In many ways food has become the new D.I.Y., the leisure pursuit of choice in millions of households. In this age of refrigerated airfreight, fast food, gourmet ready meals and the microwave, long hours spent in the preparation and cooking of food are no longer necessary – chopping, pounding, stirring, simmering and searing are done simply for fun, for relaxation and, above all, for pleasure. We are becoming masters of the culinary arts in our own homes, producing elaborate dishes which any Michelin-starred restaurant would be proud of. Traditional cooks' equipment shops are seeing an unprecedented resurgence in sales, while companies such as Bodum, Alessi, Philips and Zanussi are responding to the insatiable popular demand for 'designer' versions of basic kitchen equipment – refrigerators, ovens, kettles, toasters, oven lighters, bottle openers, salt and pepper cellars.

In a world in which we are as often defined by our tastes as by our professions, the food we choose to eat, the way we decorate our kitchens and dining rooms, and the restaurants we choose to eat at all speak volumes about how we see ourselves. Indeed, it is no coincidence that today's interest in food goes hand-in-hand with an increased awareness in style and design – or 'lifestyle' as the media-savvy would have it. Food is increasingly being used as an expression of self. It has become a mechanism to protect ourselves from an uncertain and unpredictable future where international corporations and global media threaten to turn us all into one homogeneous, choiceless and faceless nation of workers and consumers. We use food, just as we use what we wear and how we furnish our homes, as a means of retaining our sense of individuality. We also use it to create meaningful experiences in a world in which meaning seems increasingly elusive.

Food producers and retailers use marketing analysis studies of the new consumer trends to rethink their strategies in the face of fierce competition. Cult American future trend predictor Faith Popcorn has

Kitchen utensils from the Italian company Alessi. L–r: 'Twergi' salt and pepper mills by Andrea Branzi, 'Lilliput' salt and pepper shakers by Stefano Giovannoni, spice pots by Stefano Giovannoni, 'Juicy Salif' lemon squeezer by Philippe Starck, 'Gino Zucchino' sugar sifter by Guido Venturini, 'Kettle with Bird' by Michael Graves, 'Fred Worm' vacuum flask by Guido Venturini, 'Little Devil' bottle openers by Biagio Cisotti, 'Firebird' gas-lighter by Guido Venturini, 'Anna G.' corkscrew by Alessandro Mendini.

identified an increasing move towards 'anchoring' – a return to more traditionalist values in order to 'anchor' ourselves in the future; 'cocooning' – reflecting our strong desire to surround ourselves with the cosy and familiar in order to protect ourselves from the harsh, unpredictable realities of the outside world over which we have no control; and 'cashing out' – opting out of the competitive way of life and choosing a more fulfilling, simpler lifestyle. Market research such as this is eagerly consumed by those companies that bring food to our table, enabling them to become increasingly well-versed at giving us endless new opportunities to demonstrate food as lifestyle choice.

We've certainly all done it – standing in the supermarket queue peering into our neighbour's trolley and making an instant judgement about who they are. But can you define a person, their life and habits, on the basis of the groceries in their trolley? Supermarkets do – they have already categorized you. Reward cards allow the key players to accumulate data about shopping habits and keep close tabs on changing tastes and needs. Where once success in the retail world was measured by efficiency and speed in response to demand, now it's the connection with the individual – 'stroking' the customer – which supermarkets are hoping will ensure them customer loyalty. Shoppers will be made to feel they are being offered a more personal service, tailored to their individual and changing needs. Supermarkets want to enter into a 'dialogue' with their customers in order to make them feel special and valued. They are providing specialist in-store bakeries, butchers, deli counters, cafés, crèches. Tesco's new flagship store in London even boasts a sushi bar.

These great cathedrals of choice are actively building the idea of excitement back into shopping. Instead of it being a chore, a matter of ticking everything off a list and then going home exhausted, supermarkets are striving to make shopping fun, and are slowly changing to become places in which to spend time, browsing, choosing, relaxing, enjoying – and exercising the power of our plastic. The increase in home shopping – shopping on the internet or placing an order by telephone – will only contribute to this trend. Home shopping will principally account for the basic items, leaving the supermarket trip for the things we enjoy buying, for browsing and picking over the luxury items.

Restaurants, too, are registering the new consumer trends. Diners seem to be tiring of the pan-Pacific mix of increasingly exotic ingredients in elaborately designed interiors. Instead, traditional home cooking – or the 'heap' as architect Will Alsop would have it – is served in intimate surroundings with mismatched chairs, rickety tables and battered old sofas. Even the names of restaurants – Home, the Living Room, Lunch – reflect the desire to create an ambience of down-to-earth cosiness. And hence the current rash of back-to-basics cookbooks and television series – Delia Smith's *How to Cook*, Nigella Lawson's *How to Eat*, Nigel Slater's *Real Food* – which describe simple pleasures, comfort food, 'real' home cooking. Just as current notions of luxury are less about conspicuous extravagance and more about quiet, thoughtfully chosen displays of quality, so our relationship with food is now a careful blend of choices self-consciously revealing the breadth of our knowledge – in other words, our taste.

Yet our permissive search for pleasurable experiences should be treated with caution. What real benefit do we gain from out-of-season asparagus being jetted across the world at vast cost? And just how many more restaurants offering the latest in gastronomic experiences do we need? If our view of happiness is measured only by an unending search for the latest, the most fashionable, the most sensational and surprising, then we will, inevitably, be left only with a sense of dissatisfaction. As we increasingly use food to fill an emotional vacuum in our lives, we are in

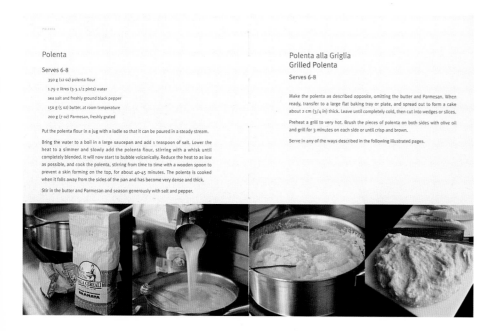

Polenta

Serves 6-8

    350 g (12 oz) polenta flour
    1.75-2 litres (3-3.1/2 pints) water
    sea salt and freshly ground black pepper
    150 g (5 oz) butter, at room temperature
    200 g (7 oz) Parmesan, freshly grated

Put the polenta flour in a jug with a ladle so that it can be poured in a steady stream.

Bring the water to a boil in a large saucepan and add 1 teaspoon of salt. Lower the heat to a simmer and slowly add the polenta flour, stirring with a whisk until completely blended. It will now start to bubble volcanically. Reduce the heat to as low as possible, and cook the polenta, stirring from time to time with a wooden spoon to prevent a skin forming on the top, for about 40-45 minutes. The polenta is cooked when it falls away from the sides of the pan and has become very dense and thick.

Stir in the butter and Parmesan and season generously with salt and pepper.

Polenta alla Griglia
Grilled Polenta

Serves 6-8

Make the polenta as described opposite, omitting the butter and Parmesan. When ready, transfer to a large flat baking tray or plate, and spread out to form a cake about 2 cm (3/4 in) thick. Leave until completely cold, then cut into wedges or slices.

Preheat a grill to very hot. Brush the pieces of polenta on both sides with olive oil and grill for 3 minutes on each side or until crisp and brown.

Serve in any of the ways described in the following illustrated pages.

The *River Café Cook Book* by Rose Gray and Ruth Rogers epitomizes the 1990s trend for the authentic peasant Italian experience.

Chips

What I want of a chip depends on my mood. A rustling pile of thin *frites* with a rare steak; a parcel of slightly soggy thick-cut chips soaked in rough vinegar on the way home from the pub; or something in between – crisp and thick and fluffy inside – for pigging out at home with hot chilli sauce or a pot of garlicky mayonnaise as a 'chip dip'. As much as I love elegant, white steamed potatoes, crunchy potato skins, or light-as-a-dream *pommes soufflées*, sometimes it just has to be chips.

The spuds should be of the big, floury variety – Maris Piper, Edwards – and need two fryings in clear, hot oil or dripping. The first to soften; the next, at a higher temperature, to crisp.

Enough for 2

4 large, floury potatoes
2 litres melted dripping or lard or sunflower oil for deep-frying

Peel the potatoes and cut them into long, thick slices, about as long and thick as your fingers. Unless you have very big hands, in which case you should aim for about 1cm in width. Leave them in cold water to stop them sticking together.

Put the fat or oil to heat in a deep pan over a low flame. Bring it slowly up to 150°C. If you don't have a kitchen thermometer, you can check by adding a chip to the oil – if it sinks, then the oil is not hot enough. If it floats in a mass of bubbles, the temperature is right. Drain the chips and dry them on a clean tea towel, then put them in a frying basket and lower them gently into the fat. They will crackle and bubble alarmingly. Let them fry for about five minutes, until they are soft but still pale. Lift out and drain. Bring the oil up to 185°C. Be very careful at this point – the fat is very dangerous (you know this, but I just want to remind you). Return the chips to the fat for three to four minutes, shaking the basket now and again to help them brown evenly.

When they are golden brown and crisp, drain briefly on kitchen paper. Salt them enthusiastically and please don't forget to turn off the fat.

35

Left: Nigel Slater's *Real Food* reflects the latest trend for a return to the simple pleasures in life – comfort food and 'real' home cooking – and includes recipes on how to cook the perfect chip. Below left: Delia Smith, her latest book, *How to Cook* (below and bottom) is a back-to-basics look at cooking, indicative of the gradual loss of cooking skills in our society.

1
All about eggs

If you want to learn how to cook, start with eggs. That's my advice. Eggs are, after all, a powerful symbol of something new happening – new life, a new beginning. But there is another reason. Somehow eggs have become an equally negative symbol. When someone says, 'Oh, I can't even boil an egg', what they are actually saying is, 'I can't cook anything at all.'

How to cook
potatoes

Opposite: Elizabeth David, the food writer credited with re-introducing the 'idea' of food to the British. Her writings and recipes brought warmth, light and colour to a world blighted by shortages and rationing. She described how to make hitherto unheard of dishes such as paella, polenta, risotto and cassoulet. But more than this, she also explained the dishes – where they came from, who cooked them, who ate them and when.

danger of losing sight of the real meaning, benefits and pleasures of food and the culture of food.

What can we expect from the kitchen of the future? Zanussi's recent report into future trends offers us a vision of a kitchen capable of running itself, where the fridge keeps track of all the family groceries, suggesting evening meals based on what is in stock and the nutritional needs of each household member, and automatically orders an extra pint of milk to be delivered when the supply runs low. And if you are having friends round for Christmas, you can decide to colour the kitchen, including all the appliances, a festive mixture of red and green at the touch of a button. The use of smart materials will allow appliances to react to their environment: the oven cavity, for example, could adjust itself automatically to the size of the meal being cooked, avoiding waste energy; the refrigerator could adjust to its content to avoid unoccupied cooling space, while the material would be infused with anti-bacterial agents to ensure food safety; and the oven front could change colour using thermo-chrome materials to indicate temperature rise, while keeping the exterior cool. Zanussi predict that in future people will desire more than just performance and aesthetic appeal from their appliances; they will expect design values in terms of sound, smell and feel, so that all their senses are aroused.

So, if the food on our plate is increasingly brought to us courtesy of science, engineering and technology, of research and development, marketing analysis, advertising and the soft-sell, where is there room for the magic embrace – the caress of the senses – which food has for so long represented? In the face of a future filled with genetically enhanced crops, foodaceuticals, quick-chill and microwave convenience, shopping via information technology and digital media, we cling to old-fashioned notions about food for reassurance. The danger here is that we may be heading towards a two-tier food system – food for nutrition and food as recreation. Cooking would be the first casualty of this. It is already changing from an everyday skill to a specialist weekend activity. Tomorrow's kitchen could be a cultural desert during the week, dispensing microwaved meals in less than 10 minutes to be eaten in front of the television, while at weekends it bristles with activity, with free-range, naturally reared and organic foodstuffs being used as part of quality recreation with family and friends. And that's only the most optimistic scenario – tomorrow's generation may simply not know how to cook. Other countries would do well to follow the example of the French school system whose syllabus includes lessons in how to taste. While British schoolchildren take classes in food technology and are taught to distinguish flavours by blind-tasting jelly babies, French schoolchildren take part in *la semaine du goût* – one week every year when some of the greatest French chefs go into schools to educate children about food, food culture and the pleasures of eating.

Food today represents opportunity. Unlike any other time in history, we have the means to control the quality of our food and our food supplies. We can ensure good food is available to the vast majority of people. Recent advances in food technology – in the production, supply and retailing of food – should be welcomed. Sophisticated supply and distribution

Above: The British magazine *Food Illustrated*, and the Australian *Vogue Entertaining & Travel* are just two of the new breed of food magazines unkindly christened 'gastroporn'.

Below: The Focus on Food Campaign – a joint initiative set up in Britain with the Royal Society of Arts aims to promote, develop and sustain the place of food education in children's learning. In 1998 500 primary schools throughout the country took part. Activities explored ways in which schools could work with specialists to extend pupils' experience of food, especially those skills associated with making food.

networks mean that supermarkets no longer have to strive for blanket national distribution, but can operate on a region-by-region basis, which allows them to stock a greater variety of fresher foods, better quality food, and more specialized and regional produce. As digital information becomes an integral part of our busy lives, we can look forward to the convenience of home shopping via the internet. And rather than automatically rejecting developments in food science, we should learn to understand and embrace them as they may help to alleviate the world's food problems, including food shortages, crop failure and famine. Certainly, we need the system of testing and monitoring that is already in place to ensure safety, but we ignore at our peril the potential and possibility that food technology offers.

The current renaissance in food and food culture should also be reassessed and re-evaluated. Rather than relentlessly pursuing the latest fad or fashion in food or, indeed, allowing ourselves to be seduced by media hype and manipulation, we should come to respect, understand and cherish the full meaning of food. Through education and example, and guided by the understanding and knowledge of a host of food writers such as Elizabeth David, we have already learned that even simple fare –

an omelette and a glass of wine – can be as delicious and enjoyable as the most intricate and expensive of dishes. The same is true of design – it doesn't need to be exclusive or expensive to bring pleasure and comfort.

Indeed, here is another parallel between food and design. Just as design, when considered superficially, can be too easily dismissed as mere style over content, the same can be said of food. A true appreciation of design encompasses an understanding of its history, its ability to change the look of our world and how we interact with it, of technological progress and creative achievement, of our understanding of ourselves and our environment. Food represents who we are, our culture and society; it feeds our senses and our emotions; it binds us together and gives us an understanding of our place in the world and of our relationship to other people. As the writer and historian Theodore Zeldin so elegantly described in his book *An Intimate History of Humanity* (1994), gastronomy is the art of creating happiness. If used correctly, he argues, focusing not on self-indulgence but on exploration, not just on self-exploration but on the exploration of the whole of nature, we can look forward to ever-widening horizons of pleasure and understanding for all people.

Elizabeth David in her kitchen. David came to represent a certain 'Provençal' style – for her, the cooking environment was as important as the ingredients used. Terence Conran, among other notable chefs and restaurateurs, readily admit their debt to her.

Food as fashion

Stephen Bayley

Two years before the birth of the Ford Transit, the start of an era if ever there was one, the first Italian pizza oven was delivered to an address in London's Soho. Soon after, Pizza Express opened in Wardour Street with decorations by Enzo Apicella. This was 1964 and the style was terracotta and spotlights, painted *Chiavari* chairs and bold graphics. As if charting London real-estate price movements, Bloomsbury followed in 1967, Fulham Road (with Paolozzi murals) in 1968 and Notting Hill Gate in 1969. Not far away, Mario & Franco were introducing a slightly higher income bracket to another style of Italian food at their Terrazza. Today, Mario's son Piero runs one of London's biggest importers of Italian tiles and floor coverings. The link between styles of food and moments in design is a strong one.

You can forget that twelve month window when Philip Larkin said sexual intercourse began: 1960s style will be as much remembered for the introduction of South European peasant food. Significantly, Habitat opened in the same year as Pizza Express. For Terence Conran and his customers it was a short step from wanting to eat Provençal ratatouille to wanting to buy and use the implements – even the entire kitchen – for making it. It is not too simplistic to see in Habitat an expression in furniture and hardware of Elizabeth David's revolution in taste which began with John Lehmann's publication of *Mediterranean Food* in 1950. The illustrations were by John Minton, and with their fishermen's balls, check tablecloths and rough implements predicted (or perhaps 'directed') bistro style. There is always a direct link between the food we eat and the place we eat it.

The march of modern sensibility throughout Britain can be charted by the spread of margheritas and butcher's blocks. Habitat Manchester opened in 1967; Findus started selling deep-frozen lasagne in 1972 (43 years after Heinz first offered spaghetti in tins). My own first memories of pizza are themselves forever associated with abstract art. It was in the house of Jules Lubbock, a generous and outgoing young teacher at Manchester

Right and bottom: The prawn cocktail and avocado pear, both stylish Continental introductions to the 1960s menu, became the staple starters of the 1970s and something of a cliché.

Top left and right: The kiwi fruit was the ubiquitous garnish of the 1980s – seen in everything from fruit salads to sandwiches.

University, that I was first served pizza (pronounced the Italian way with a very short 'i') in 1971 in an environment stuffed with bright Josef Albers prints. Thus, for me as an individual, the loop between pizza and modernism was confirmed.

Still on a larger stage this relationship endures. Italian food seems inseparable from social and cultural progress. As a child I was a regular at a theatreland restaurant called Topo Gigio, then in Great Windmill Street, long since removed in much diminished style to Great Pulteney Street. Here I would eat avocado (always in those days erroneously known in a gesture of suburban refinement and redundant amplification as avocado 'pear') with prawn cocktail followed by the sempiternal *cotoletta milanese*, in its fire blanket version. But just as the repertoire of Italian cooking has advanced, so has interior design. The old Topo Gigio had lots of velour and dark wood and neon. It would be just as unthinkable to be served an avocado 'pear' in the harsh environment of Richard Rogers' industrial River Café as it would be to eat a Ruth Rogers signature dish of, say, barely transformed butterflied lamb with charred *rosmarino* in surroundings of pompous luxury.

Not only dishes but basic ingredients continuously evolve. Consider, for instance, the curious history of the kiwi fruit or Chinese gooseberry. Twenty-five years ago the kiwi fruit was a genuine exotic, a tropical rarity revered – perhaps – by Polynesians in fertility rituals, but an anomaly in a suburban fruit basket whose familiar residents were unripe bananas and a Golden Delicious tasting like sweetened carpet underlay. Moved by government subsidies rather than any very elevated gastronomic initiative, New Zealand farmers started cultivating the kiwi fruit and successfully promoted it as a valuable source of vitamin C. Slowly, the hideous kiwi infiltrated fruit salads at just the time when the fruity salad was itself becoming an area for adventurous experimentation by chefs both domestic and professional.

At about the same time, *French cooking* – or, at least, French professional cooking – was undergoing one of its frequent revolutions. Cuisine minceur sought to radicalize both the substance and the appearance of what was on the plate. In place of heartily satisfying starch, the eater had to take his pleasure from daring combinations of flavours (rhubarb and venison, kippers and kumquats, that sort of thing) and here the kiwi found its true role ... as decoration. Being firm fleshed, the kiwi was easy to slice in the approved fashion, and being a sort of fluorescent swamp green, it animated the plate. Suddenly, slices of kiwi were everywhere: a sloppy shorthand for 'sophistication'. Kiwi became *garni*, assuming the role that previous generations had reserved for a sprig of cress or a hemisphere of tomato cut to look like a rose.

In matters of fashion things soon pass from being outrageous to familiar to old hat. This has happened to the kiwi. Its presence in the limelight of sophistication was a very brief one indeed and it is now in fashionable decline, a process that will be confirmed as soon as we see kiwi-flavoured crisps. To serve a kiwi fruit today in any form would be brazenly to declare one's naiveté or gullibility, one's complete ignorance of fashion ... or, you might say, to declare one's resistance to fashion and one's brave and independent spirit. It is at this point that the kiwi may yet be ready for

Left: The modern 'Trattoria' style of the 1960s and 1970s was a refreshing alternative to the dark, claustrophobic interiors of most post-war restaurants. The new decor brought in light and clean lines, using quarry-tile floors, spotlights and modern chairs – in this case 'Tulip' chairs and a table by Eero Saarinen.

Above: Habitat was opened by Terence Conran in 1964. Conran drew inspiration from Elizabeth David, as well as his own travels in Italy and the south of France. He introduced a fresh look to the homes and kitchens of trendy young Britons selling classic cookware, glass and crockery; terracottas, enamel and earthenware.

an ironic revival. The same wholesale fruit merchant who introduced the kiwi fruit to Britain had, a generation before, also presided at the coming out of that other useless middle-class vegetable, the courgette.

Fashions in food tend to follow this pattern, a familiar curve that could easily be demonstrated graphically. Take garlic. Garlic had political origins. The post-Revolutionary National Assembly influenced the import into Paris of a wide variety of regional dishes. The influence of Provence was the strongest, and the Deputies arriving in the capital from the south not only brought with them Rouget de l'Isle's inspiring anthem, but also the Marseillaise taste for cooking in oil and with garlic. By the time garlic had been established in Paris for nearly a century, it was still causing trouble to English visitors. In 1875 Thomas King Chambers published his *Manual of Diet in Health and Disease*. He wrote of a favourite member of the genus Allium:

Another article of cuisine that offends the bowels of unused Britons is garlic. Not uncommonly in southern climes an egg with the shell on is the only procurable animal food without garlic in it. Flatulence and looseness are the frequent results. Bouilli, with its accompaniments of mustard sauce and water melon, is the safest resource and not an unpleasant one ... after a little education.

Yet a mere 70 years later Elizabeth David was composing *Mediterranean Food* and garlic had achieved almost mystical status. To invoke it and other southern ingredients was a form of pornography (since it stimulated what at the time were considered unwholesome cravings). Referring to the drab days after the Second World War, Mrs David wrote (and you can imagine the heavy breathing):

I sat down and ... started to work out an agonised craving for the sun and a furious revolt against that terrible, cheerless, heartless food, by writing down descriptions of Mediterranean and Middle Eastern cooking. Even to write words like apricot, olives and butter, rice and lemons, oil and almonds, produced assuagement. Later I came to realise that in the England of 1947, those were dirty words. (*Mediterranean Food*, 1950)

Just yesterday, at my children's school there was an overwhelming smell of garlic. My daughter explained to me that they have garlic bread for lunch everyday. And taramasalata and lasagne. My own memories of childhood salads include hatchet-cut grey eggs and depressed lettuce leaves, both limp and dry and quite undressed. My son and daughter can make their own vinaigrette (using Elizabeth David's recipe) and are at least as a familiar with arugula as I was with cucumber segments.

Wine is another example of the astonishing changes in sophistication in the consumer. In 1948 Marcel Boulestin (the first television chef) told a story about having dinner in the house of a Member of Parliament. He said that the *white wine was so incredibly bad that, pretending to be interested in it, I asked its name. My hostess did not know it, nor did the parlour maid, who went to the pantry to look at the bottle.* (*Ease and Endurance*, 1948)

Today, I would say the ordinary English consumer has a better general knowledge of wine than anyone else on earth, especially the French (who are quite exceptionally ignorant in this area). Recently a policeman came to visit us at home after one of the break-ins that are a ritual in the area where we live. I offered him a glass of wine which he accepted. He held it up to the light, smelt the volatiles and the swirled the glass to nose the secondaries. He tasted it cautiously, rushing it in and out of his teeth and over the tongue to excite the taste buds. 'Côtes du Rhone?' he asked and he was absolutely right. In a Blur song 'Beaujolais' is used to rhyme with 'way'. Gazza may enjoy a Flaming Lamborghini (which *The Sun* explains is a hellish mixture of Kahlua, Curaçao, Baileys, Tequila, Premium Lead Free and Vimto), but everyone else prefers a pleasant glass of lightly chilled Sauvignon.

And, of course, appetites change with fashions, or maybe it is the other way around. For certain, the 'design' of meals has changed. In his *Ramble Through Normandy* of 1855 George Musgrave described a picnic lunch for two. It consisted of soup, fried mackerel, beefsteak, French beans, fried potatoes, omelette fines herbes, a fricandeau of veal with sorrel, a roast chicken garnished with mushrooms, a hock of pork served on spinach, an apricot tart, three custards, an endive salad, a small roast leg of lamb with chopped onion and nutmeg, coffee, absinthe, eau dorée, a Mignon cheese, pears, plums, grapes, cakes and two bottles of red Burgundy, one of white. The same couple today would probably eat a rocket salad with a shaving of parmesan and a little grilled fish, perhaps with a spritzer.

Taste is not universal. It is culturally and socially conditioned. There is no known group of humans who eat everything available to them. A comestible greatly admired by one group is often detested by another. Mrs Beeton, the Delia Smith of her day, had a recipe for 'Fishklosh', roast wallaby and parrot pie. The natives of Brunei prize rotten eggs as a delicacy, just as the English sportsman enjoys having his game putrefy before cooking it. Navajo Indians believe fresh fish is poisonous, and a number of important dishes in classical Arab cookery depend on a dough made of rotten barley, known to contain aflatoxins, among the deadliest carcinogens.

Historians know that taste tends to move from a general preference for 'sweet' to 'dry'. We are now in a dry phase. If you don't believe me, ask a wine merchant about sales of amontillado in comparison with brut champagne. Yet at Vauxhall Pleasure Gardens (fl.1661–1859), while champagne was available for eight shillings a bottle, most visitors preferred 'Vauxhall Nectar', an emetic concoction of rum, syrup and petals of benjamin flowers. German wines were sold with added sugar.

Patterns in cooking are just as cyclical, a period of excess being followed by a period of austerity. Elizabeth David's glorious cycle of books began when she started longing for exotic ingredients during the drab days of

Above: Hard-boiled duck embryos. Novices eat them with lights dimmed. Balut, Philippines. Left: Wildlife as food – rats grilled whole, with tails, over an open fire, served on green leaves. Southern Province, Sierra Leone. Below: The legendary cook and restaurateur Robert Carrier guided a generation of aspirant novice cooks through the intricacies of cooking, from the preliminary basics to the peaks of haute cuisine.

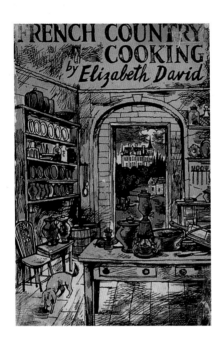

Left: Elizabeth David, *French Country Cooking* with illustrations by John Minton. A seminal book, David's second, published in 1953 after the success of *Mediterranean Food*, punctured the myth that all French cooking was heavy and cream-laden. The illustrations reflected David's own taste and inspired the fashion for the 'rustic' look.
Below: A strip from Len Deighton's *Où est Le Garlic?*, 1965. Based on Deighton's famous cookstrips for *The Observer*. Deighton's no-nonsense approach reflected a new-found glamour for men to be able to rustle up sophisticated dinners in no time and with very little effort. Deighton offered such 'bachelor quickies' as two-minute Lobster bisque made from a tin of condensed chicken soup and a tin of lobster.

rationing when you were lucky to get beige soup or a rubbery rissole, never mind pissaladière or ratatouille. Mrs David's instruction (adapted from Escoffier) to 'Faites simple!' was a moral and aesthetic instruction as much as a culinary one. And here we are approaching a definition. To understand food and fashion, you have to appreciate that cooking and design have a lot in common. A good design must have a sound concept, fine ingredients, be well made. It should be functional and it should, if at all possible, be pleasant to look at. Similarly, good cooking must also have excellent ingredients and preparation and should follow a reliable recipe. The result should be both nutritious and flavoursome. That's fine, but within those rules, there's huge room for variety.

In any society evolved beyond (a) rationing or (b) subsistence, food is a matter for social competition, for cultural modelling. Jean Anthelme Brillat-Savarin said 'tell me what you eat and I'll tell you what you are' (*Physiologies du gout*). He was right, but should have added ... 'and what you want to be'. It is in formal French cooking that the expression 'good taste' first appears, originally as a means of putting down the peasantry and their coarse preferences. Social competition was intense in eighteenth-century France. The Marquis d'Uxelles gave his name to a dish of quails in mushroom sauce, still in the classical repertoire as *cailles à la duxelles*. Another famous dish, *Filet de volailles à la Bellevue*, was named by Mdme De Pompadour after one of her favourite houses. Louis XV made his own omelettes. *Boeuf Stroganoff* was named for a Russian prince. These were dishes that were 'designed': deliberate gestures of taste with a 'brand' attached.

Thanks to a large degree to Elizabeth David, food became a matter of fashion in post-war Britain. Just as during the 1950s the Council of Industrial Design wanted to save English taste through Scandinavian furniture, so Elizabeth David and her followers sought to do the same

Opposite: Pages from the *Life Picture Cook Book* (1961) which broke new ground in introducing the idea of 'lifestyle' cooking as part of a hectic schedule of entertaining. Men and women were given distinct roles – steak was a 'man's job', as was the dangerous art of the flambé, while women were charged with preparing hors-d'oeuvres for cocktail parties and clam chowder for informal supper parties.

MAN'S JOB: STEAK

WHENEVER the menu calls for a delicate dish or a fancy pie, most men are more than happy to let their wives take care of the cooking. When it's a matter of steak, this tolerant attitude is replaced by an unassailable belief in masculine know-how. Steak is a man's job.

But steak chefs are a divided clan, full of stubborn preferences. They disagree as to the perfect cut—whether porterhouse, sirloin or filet. They argue about how to cook it. Some, like Quincy Jones, shown on the opposite page, char the steak first, then grill it slowly. Others do it just the other way around. Some connoisseurs go in for spreads and sauces. Others insist on nothing but salt on their steaks. And among the purists, the relative merits of charcoal and wood fires can stir up a storm like the one that brews in Kentucky when the discussion turns to crushing or bruising the mint in a julep.

In the wood-burning faction, many like to use hickory or fruitwoods to give a special taste to the steak. The perfect wood fire should be built just big enough to burn down to a four-inch bed of coals which, when spread evenly, is slightly larger than the steak itself. The fire is ready when the coals are glowing and have a light film of white ash. For the charcoal faction, the small, uniform, top quality briquets will give the best performance. Two dozen should be enough for a medium-size grill. Broiling with charcoal takes less time and fewer briquets than used by most amateur chefs.

The time it takes to cook a steak over an open fire depends not only on the thickness of the steak, but also on four highly variable conditions: the temperature of the steak, how hot the fire is, the temperature of the air and the strength of the drafts or breezes. As a rule of thumb, if a 1½-inch steak is at room temperature and placed about 6 inches from a good bed of coals, it should be rare after 5 minutes on each side, medium rare at 6 minutes, and well done at 10 minutes per side. The surest method is to test the steak just before the allotted time by making a small cut near the center and judging by color. But meat continues to cook for a while after removal from the fire, and the stickler for an exact degree of rareness should stop when the color is still a bit too red.

An outdoor charcoal grill is mounted in the living room of Architect Quincy Jones's Los Angeles home. Here Jones broils individual porterhouse steaks, charring them first, then grilling them slowly.

Individual porterhouse steaks should look like these—not too thick, bright red, fine-grained, firm, marbled with fat. Jones, who sides with the sauce-lovers, will serve these with Western Herb Sauce.

FLAMING FOOD

ONE of the most festive ways to entertain formally is to cook, or finish cooking, the food right on the table, before the guests' eyes. It is also one of the most practical. Quick, hot, on-the-scene preparation improves the flavor of many good dishes and whets the appetite of the diners while adding drama to the occasion.

The most spectacular method, of course, is to flame the food itself, in a chafing dish or in a platter or on a skewer that can be as fancy as the dagger shown on the opposite page. The real purpose of serving food *flambé* is to add a final fillip to a dish which has already been cooked in a chafing dish or prepared in the kitchen. To flame the food use distilled spirits like brandy, whisky, gin, rum or kirsch—a good domestic brandy will do as well as a fine cognac. First warm a spoon over a match or candle. Pour in the liquor, light it and pour it on the food. The warm spoon makes the liquor light readily and does away with those fizzled-out matchsticks sometimes found floating in the platter. By the time the flame has gone out the food will have absorbed the taste of the liquor, as well as some of its zip.

A commoner method is to use a chafing dish for on-the-table cooking. Back in the '20s these dishes were mainly used for such niceties as fudge or Welsh rarebit, but today they are being put to work in many maidless households to make or warm more solid fare. Because it can keep food warm as well as cook it, the chafing dish is ideal to use at teen-age parties, after football games or at any meal where guests are apt to drift in late. Basically the chafing dish is a pan on a stand over a heater. The pan can be copper, brass, silver, pottery or aluminum, as plain or fancy, cheap or expensive as you like. Some chafing dishes, primarily used to warm food for serving, are heated by candles or alcohol lamps. Others, which do more actual cooking, use canned heat or electricity.

Some of the dishes shown on the next three pages, like the Swiss fondue and sukiyaki, are best when actually cooked at the table. Others, like the chipped beef in mushroom sauce and Mexican corn casserole, can be kept warm for hours on end. And the rest, like the flaming duck or kippers, are eye-catching when served *flambé*.

With a ball of brandy-soaked cotton flaming at its tip, a handsome dagger pierces a tomato and beef collops interspersed with mushrooms and pieces of green pepper. Before they were flamed on the dagger, collops and vegetables were cooked on a skewer over hot coals in the brazier at upper right. At lower left peach halves flame in brandy in a copper pan over an alcohol stove.

Previous left page: The Galloping Gourmet, Australian flamboyant Graham Kerr, was something of a role model to a generation of young men for whom being able to cook cordon bleu dishes had become a sign of masculine sophistication. A favourite recipe was flambéd steak au poivre, another was poached eggs in Chartreuse sauce. Roland Barthes, in a 1972 essay on ornamental cookery, noted the post-war tendency of disguising the true nature of foodstuffs with complicated sauces. Previous right page: Husband and wife team Johnny and Fanny Craddock were among the first of a new breed of British television cooks. Fanny's fur stoles, décolleté necklines and playful tyranny over her dinner-jacketed husband brought a comedy of cordon bleu manners to millions of homes. Right: Chef Michel Guérard in Eugénie-les-Bains, his flagship restaurant in rural Gascony (below).

with robust southern European peasant food. There is a curious precedent to this politicization of ingredients. The word 'restaurant' first appears in the stories of Marguerite de Navarre where it means a restorative soup. By 1771 it had entered the *Dictionnaire de Trévoux* where it was explained thus: 'Certain *traiteurs* in Paris who sell nothing but *restaurants* are called *restaurateurs*'. In pre-Revolutionary Paris, you had to expect to eat in a private house. The restaurant became established as an institution when, after the French Revolution, cooks left the great houses and set up independently. At just the same time, they were able to become celebrities. (It was the same in music: while Haydn had been a tradesman/servant, Beethoven was an artistic genius.) The original restaurant was, if you like, the very first 'consumer' experience in that it was a service offered for sale to complete strangers (whereas hitherto food had been the subject of master–servant or family relationships). People learn about interior design from the experience of going to restaurants where the style of the food served is always in some sort of relationship to the environment. If you were going to eat *tournedos rossini or escalope de veau Holstein* or if you had a bit of a hankering for a crêpe Suzette you would want to satisfy it in an environment defined by burgundy velour banquettes, pink napery and copper chafing dishes. Your *tournedos rossini* would look very odd in a galvanized angle-iron neo-Modern environment lit by low-voltage dichroic lamps. Equally, a chaste modern dish – say grilled sardines – would be best appreciated in a very particular environment. Food and interior design are both expressions of taste ... and of fashion.

It was Michel Guérard's *La Grande Cuisine Minceur* of 1976 that codified nouvelle cuisine and offers us perhaps the most complete example of fashion in food, a business of supreme artifice. Fashion is, by definition, unnecessary, which is what makes it so fascinating. It is necessary for fashion to create demand. Hence the absurd novelties of cuisine minceur. Conceptual inversions were de rigueur. Starters had to be given the names of puddings and vice versa. Thus *sorbet de fromage de tête*. Main courses confused appellations of meat and fish: *rumsteck de sole*. The same with vegetables: *gâteau de carottes*. Entrées were given the names of starters: *soupe de figues*. In *Un Festinen Paroles* (1979) Jean-François Revel sighed of an eighteenth-century dish:

Faut-il considérer ... Le canard aux huîtres comme une survivance medievale ou un anticipation moderne ... on ne sait. (Should we think of ... duck with oysters as a medieval survival or a prediction of something modern ... one doesn't know)

But Guérard also furnishes me with one anecdote that explains precisely the absurd relationship between food and fashion. Eugénie-les-Bains is Guérard's flagship restaurant, a splendid Empire-style building in rural Gascony. Here M. Guérard practised his artifice to the delight of Michelin inspectors who gave him three rosettes to demonstrate their respect. A year or so ago, I booked a family lunch there, preceded by an exchange of letters, phone calls and faxes. We arrived at the due time, only to find there had been a mistake. Madame was flustered as she explained the problem. We watched fat Belgian millionaires and their thin mistresses

shuffle in for a 300-calorie lunch. Madame wanted to know if we realized
that M. Guérard had opened another restaurant around the back? La Ferme
aux Grives was a revelation. Napoleonic splendour gave way to peasant
style. 300 calories gave way to a very *grande bouffe*. No menu. No minceur.
A jug of wine, a tub of pâté, an omelette, a *daube*, a salad, a rich pudding,
cheese, more wine. A roaring fire and tables groaning with produce. No fat
Belgian millionaires.

There is more choice and meaning in the selection, preparation and
consumption of food than in any other activity. Brillat-Savarin was correct:
tell him what you eat and he will tell you what you are. Tell him where you
eat and the conclusion will be the same. Fashion and food are expressions
of the continuous human search for quality and variety. But one word
of warning. Pierre Gagnaire recently ran a remarkable restaurant in St-
Étienne where the modern art and architecture were as impressive as the
dizzily sophisticated food which won him three rosettes. The American
gourmet magazines found him, made him and turned him into a
destination restaurant for rich Texan dentists. Michelin gave him three
rosettes. And then he closed down. It was the first time this had ever
happened to a three-rosette establishment. Gagnaire said people did not
want that kind of food any more. Well, he was wrong. He was just not in the
right place. And now he has opened again in Paris, to just as much acclaim.

Everyone knows that there has been a revolution in British restaurants
the past ten years. But I wonder whether there is not another revolution in
preparation. Conran's first shops were inspired by Design Research in

Boston. His restaurants were inspired by the old established brasseries of
Paris, where there was a bright democracy of taste. Thus Pierre Andrieu in
Fine Bouche (1956):

*La Coupole ... is open day and night; one enters or leaves at pleasure
untroubled by obsequious flunkeys ... The immense room ... is blazing with
lights, the walls are decorated with paintings by loyal Montparnassians, and
the whole affords a sense of ease and comfort, a feeling of being at liberty to
do exactly as one likes. All languages are to be heard, people of every race to
be met, the place is a world in miniature that eats and drinks, reads and talks,
dreams or makes love, just as it wants.*

But Conran's London restaurants, like Habitat, had their precedents in
the US where a rash of busy, top-quality mega-restaurants, including Café
des Artistes, Luxembourg and Odeon, opened on New York's Upper East
Side in the late 1970s and early 1980s. Now they are in London, but there
may be early signs that the public is becoming fatigued by their formulaic
brightness. Peter Murray, the distinguished architectural publisher, and
I had a recent exchange about a rendezvous for lunch. With all of London
available, we thought for a moment and agreed that we didn't want to
go anywhere large and noisy. We wanted to go somewhere quiet and
intimate. 'Not' Peter said, 'anywhere modern'. I thought at the time that
I was very glad no one had overheard our conversation, but then I realized
how significant it was. Don't ask me how it happened, but at least as far
as restaurants are concerned, 'modern' is no longer sophisticated. There
has been another change in taste. But the Ford Transit is still going strong.

Previous pages and left: Quaglino's, London. This Terence Conran restaurant features specially designed furniture, lighting, china, glassware and even ashtrays. Staff uniforms were designed by Jasper Conran and inspired by French restaurants of the 1940s.

Above: Downstairs in Terence Conran's Mezzo restaurant in Soho, London. The cuisine, under the direction of chef John Torode, is a fusion of East and West, northern and southern hemispheres. In the words of Terence Conran, 'We wanted to bring something that was new and exciting to Soho, whilst staying true to the character of this part of London that is celebrated for its cosmopolitan free spirit'.

Opposite: Oxo Tower, London. A diner's view out over the River Thames from this eighth floor restaurant by architects Lifschutz Davidson. Diners are seated on leather-upholstered Charles Eames chairs.

Bar Italia, London. A family-run business which has been going for over 60 years. From the 1950s it was the centre of the Soho coffee bar cultural scene and remains so today.

Quo Vadis, London. Re-opened in 1997 as a collaboration between artist Damien Hirst, chef Marco-Pierre White and others. Contemporary art decorates the interior.

Pharmacy Bar and Grill, London. Ground floor (left) and first floor (below). Artist Damien Hirst designed the premises in collaboration with designer Mike Rundell and typographer Jonathan Barnbrook. The interior features several pieces of Hirst's art – such as his spot and butterfly paintings. The downstairs area looks like a Continental pharmacy, with glass-fronted medicine cabinets as a backdrop. Furniture consultant Jasper Morrison designed stool seats in the shape of pills to continue the pharmaceutical theme.

Above: Pharmacy– to produce a radically different façade all visual distractions were removed to leave a flat white surface as a 'frame' for the artwork inside, including the model of a DNA helix in the upstairs front window.

Chapter two

Design bites

Paola Antonelli

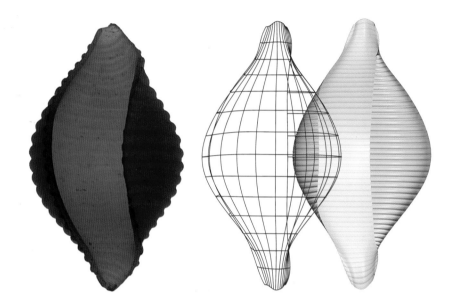

In the culminating scene of the sublime movie *Big Night*, brothers and restaurateurs Stanley Tucci and Tony Shalhoub gently extract their edible masterpiece, the timpano, from its mould, as if they were delivering a baby. They observe it, they smell it, they gently slap it to test its perfection, and they carry it on a throne to the dinner table, where they are saluted by an explosion of applause. The monumental timpano, an architectural form made, among other ingredients, of eggs, meat, tomatoes, cheese and, most important, ziti, can show designers the way to the new world. Basic foods, the fundamental units of composition in regional cuisines, are a delicious example of great design. As the design profession is looking for a new, well-defined identity in the age of bundling and multimedia, it is worth going back to the most basic forms of design for inspiration. Some everyday objects, especially the ones that are most taken for granted, like paper clips or even spaghetti, can in fact speak about the timeless role of industrial design, the timely appropriateness of innovative craftsmanship, and the continuous guidance that material culture can provide.

Some of the basic elements of gastronomical architecture are simple design objects. Some of them, moreover, have been updated from a hand-crafted tradition and are now produced industrially, with advanced automated manufacturing techniques, in numbers that surpass any other design product. A typological division of basic foods can clarify the parallel with architecture and design. Breads, for instance, can be easily subdivided according to design considerations, and can range from flat support breads – such as focaccia and pizza, pancakes, waffles, matzoth, blinis, pittas, *pão de quejo* and naan – to constructed envelopes – such as samosas, calzoni, patties, wraps, burritos and crêpes – all the way to iconic, autonomous shapes – such as croissants, pretzels and bagels. Some other foods, one degree higher in complexity, can be appreciated according to their mechanized manufacturing process – like hamburgers, hot dogs,

doughnuts, fortune cookies, potato chips. Many snacks and cereals were created in the high-tech era and provide examples of exquisitely sophisticated manufacturing processes.

Pasta, for instance, has existed for many centuries and is an example of great industrial design in which each single form solves a different function. Pasta, in all its different shapes, passes all the tests of a good design object. The simple mixture of durum wheat flour and water, shaped or extruded by hand or machine, is a perfect reference for the design discourse and can be easily approached from all critical angles. Some examples: first of all, pasta is historically an outstanding case of direct balance of means – the scarcely available resources in poor countries – and goals – the human need, nonetheless, for a somewhat diversified diet. It is such a simple and strong design idea that it has been able to generate an endless variety of derivative designs – the various types of pasta and the dishes made of them. Moreover, it is a timeless design, in that its production tools have been updated across the centuries but its basic form has remained the same. It is also a global design, easy to appropriate and adapt to local culture. As a matter of fact, almost each country has its own autonomous pasta dishes, and pasta has become the unit of the composition for more complex foods. It is a universal success with critic and public, thus passing also the marketing-driven design test. It exemplifies the zero degree of the design discourse, because it is an example of form coinciding with function. It is nonetheless somewhat resistant to merely formal manipulation, as demonstrated by several unfortunate attempts made by renowned designers. It is a design born out of necessity.

Like some other examples of great design, pasta does not have one author's name attached but many, the names of all the innovators who have improved its tradition. As a matter of fact, the Chinese and the Italians

are still arguing over the copyright of noodles. Though some claim that Marco Polo brought noodles back with him to Italy from China in the late thirteenth century, pasta already existed in both places long before. Archaeologists have found signs of Etruscan pasta dating from the fourth century B.C., and the Chinese were making a noodle-like food as early as 3000 B.C. The manufacturing process is rather simple and consistent. Italian pasta, in particular, is made of semolina, produced by grinding kernels of durum wheat and sometimes mixing it with other hard wheats or with egg. The semolina is mixed with water until it forms a dough, and the dough is then kneaded to the correct consistency. It is then pushed, or extruded, through a metallic die whose holes determine the final shape. When the extruded pasta reaches the right length, it is cut with sharp blades that rotate beneath the die. In another process, the dough is thinned by mechanical cylinders to a large sheet, and the shapes, like tagliatelle or lasagne, are cut from it. Some pasta is then further manipulated, for instance curled, as in extruded fusilli, or pinched in the middle, as in the die-cut farfalle (bow ties). The pasta is then put through large driers or is consumed fresh.

The hundreds of different types of pasta that can be obtained through these processes have different characteristics, some objectively described, others so subtle that only palates can detect them. The first, simpler classification is in relationship to their length: pasta can be long, short or extra short for soups. Soup pastas are often die-cut from sheets of egg-based dough. A second classification relates to the sauce that will be used. Popular tradition destines thinner pasta, such as thin spaghetti and capelli d'angelo (angel hair) to lighter, more liquid sauces, while thicker pasta, like fusilli and pappardelle, is more suitable for thicker sauces. Pasta with holes, like macaroni and penne, seems to respond well to chunky sauces, as well as casseroles. When it is ribbed, as in rigatoni, it absorbs the sauce rather

Right: Advertisement for various types of pasta. In all its different shapes, pasta is an excellent example of form following function, designed to be eaten with certain foods and sauces and fulfilling a specific function.

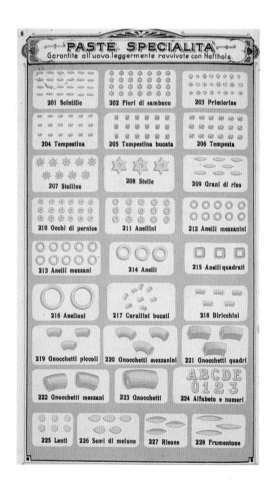

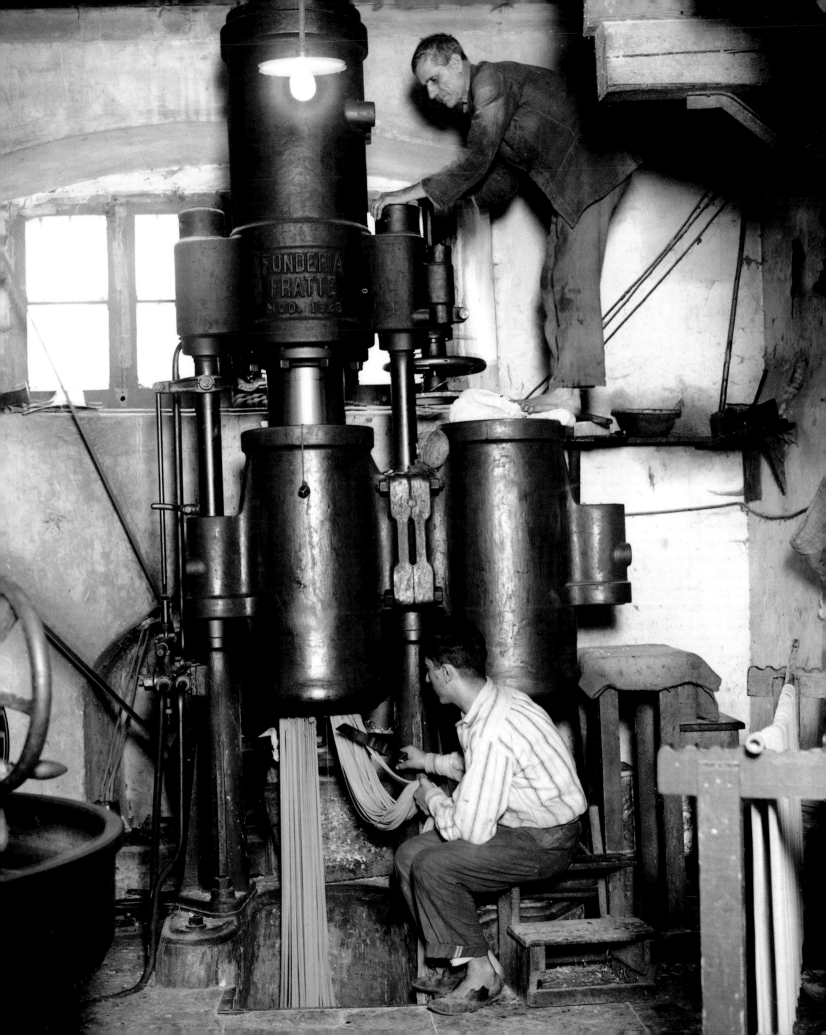

Above: Still from *Big Night*, directed by Campbell Scott and Stanley Tucci (1996). Restaurateurs Stanley Tucci and Tony Shalhoub construct the perfect timpano – a sculptural pasta casserole made from eggs, meat, tomatoes, cheese and ziti (a cross between spaghetti and macaroni). Right: Baby on a pasta shell from a 1931 Barilla calendar drawn by painter and graphic designer Adolfo Busi.

than simply being enveloped by it. Rules, nonetheless, often exist to be questioned, and it so happens that spaghetti can be the best choice for the chunkiest sauces, for instance in a seafood dish. Ultimately, each shape of pasta has its own character and some pasta recipe books become design instruction manuals.

Throughout history, pasta manufacturers have introduced new shapes, some of them very successful, but most of them quickly dismissed by the public. A few years ago the famous Barilla company added to its hundred-plus catalogue two new pastas, 'bifore' – shaped and ribbed like a brick and so-called because of its resemblance to the medieval architectural windows – and 'trifogli' – spaghetti with a three-leaf clover section. These were two tasty variations based on the honest desire to innovate the design by means of newly available technologies, but the new shapes did not encounter the public's universal favour. Most of all, pasta seems to resist any kind of signature design. Many have tried, from the French design company Nemo to visionary Luigi Colani, with no success. The 'marille', the short – and short-lived – pasta designed in 1983 by Giorgio Giugiaro for the Voiello company, which is today the skunkwork division of Barilla, is one of the most infamous examples. Giugiaro, having designed the Volkswagen Rabbit and the Fiat Panda among other cars, was at that time a hot signature and he was just taking his first steps outside of the automobile industry. Here is the story, in the designer's words, excerpted from an interview conducted by the author in 1991 at Giugiaro's headquarters in Moncalieri:

'The Voiello company had very clear ideas in mind: either the pasta would be designed by a "technological" designer such as Giugiaro, and thus be produced by means of a new type of extrusion moulding, or it would be poorly and simply shaped, and in that case they would chose Bruno Munari. We presented twelve designs, they chose five and passed them on

to product engineers. We were invited to Naples in a fancy restaurant: the pasta had been tested with all kinds of sauces. As far as the requirements, the pasta should not absorb too much sauce; it should increase its volume in water, in the sense that a dish of marille should weigh half as much as a dish of spaghetti; at the dawn of nouvelle cuisine, it should be decorative, "architectural"; it should, like all pastas, retain the sauce and let the water go; it should then be "palatable", a technical term which indicates a positive reaction of the mouth to its taste. They organized a big *vernissage* in Milano at the Centrodomus; Mendini did the design. It was a good image campaign, for the company and for its president, but the production did not go on long enough. The pasta was only distributed in a few places and people were not able to find it. Moreover, it took a few more minutes to cook and this was a discrimination point. But I owe my popular fame to that pasta, I even got published in *Newsweek*, isn't it funny?'

Giugiaro's adventure is emblematic. It seems as though innovation, especially when applied to objects born out of necessity – the ones where form and function easily coincide, like pasta or communication design – also has to follow some rules. It has to be a meaningful innovation, and not merely a formal exercise for the sake of novelty. It has to fit within the boundaries of human comfort. It has to be a systemic revolution, which guides people gently towards the new, and not a disruptive one. The simple example of pasta can prove useful when tackling the newest forms of design, such as the design of communication and information, which deal with the oldest of concepts. As technology sparks the innovation, it is up to design to be the mediator between new technology and the human world.

Food is an ode to human creativity applied to design and architecture. Not unlike a Chinese spring roll or a New Orleans gumbo, the timpano from *Big Night* is an example of a recipe that is naturally translated from

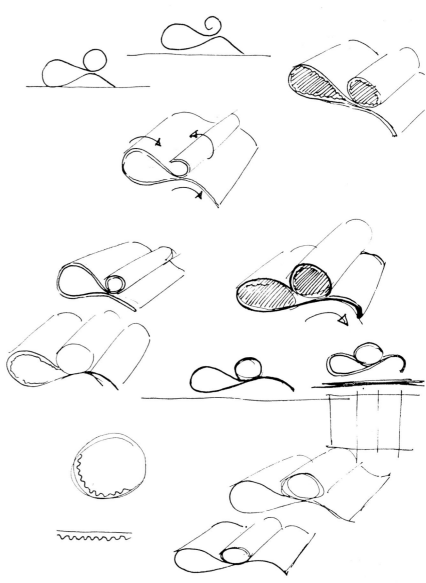

Above: Bifore and trifogli, two new pasta shapes introduced by Barilla in an attempt to utilize newly available technology. They failed to impress the buying public.

Right: The marille – designed by Italian Giorgio Giugiaro, better-known for his stylish car designs – also failed to gain popular acceptance.

generation to generation. Much like the architectural scheme of a vernacular local dwelling, it is based on the composition of some immutable elements dictated by the region's material culture, and it can then be mutated by contemporary popular culture and innovation. About 15 years ago, gastronomy also went through its modernist age. A few selected chefs around the world embraced the less-is-more religion of nouvelle cuisine. These chefs would honour their guests with oversized, preciously decorated porcelain plates featuring, for instance, a two-shrimp arch cemented with *wasabi*, resplendent over a bed made of five sumptuous chicken kidneys, and crowned by two mint leaves, and with other dishes as noble and as elegantly cool as the Barcelona Pavilion. Lately, as is happening in product design worldwide, regional tradition is often contaminated with foreign suggestions. In fusion cuisine, a Japanese tuna *sashimi* can sit on top of a fragrant medallion of *risotto alla milanese* – tasted at Nobu in New York – in mutant concoctions that at times recall some odd West Coast garage-made vehicles – half cars, half surfboards. Chefs can be compared not only to artists, but also to powerful designers. Lately, however, a resurgence of regional and national cuisine has encouraged the public to appreciate local authenticity and to seek it

as a way to acquire knowledge and experience the world.

Similarly, in architecture and design, now that modernism has ceased to be a dogma to fight against, local currents and trends have become important ways to look at the world as a whole. Different local phenomena seem to have commanded the scene at different times. Just as American and Scandinavian design were the best representation of the economical and organic 1950s, and Italy became the symbol of the power of fantasy and of the creative technological boom of the 1960s, the late 1990s also has its representatives, although the picture, just like the whole planet, is now more multifaceted and blurred by the media. As in fashion, where all revivals of different eras have been fully exploited, what matters today is not strictly provenance, but rather the authenticity and success of the composition. The postmodern activity of companies like Alessi and mail shopping catalogues like La Redoute exemplifies a new way to design, also more attuned to the fashion industry, based on the concept of 'collection' and focused on the designers' signatures, supported by the company's well-studied image. While Europe is struggling and pushing the envelope in order to discover a continental culture, its designers and architects are translating that tension into outstanding objects and buildings that

Expressionism

Farfalle and fusilli are elaborate, short pastas. The farfalle (butterflies) are die-cut from a sheet of dough and then pinched in the middle to form a bowtie, while the fusilli (little fuses) are extruded and then curled. Both are suitable for thick, chunky sauces, e.g., meat sauce or a sauce of peas, cream and ham. Liquidy sauces would be too easily absorbed within their curves.

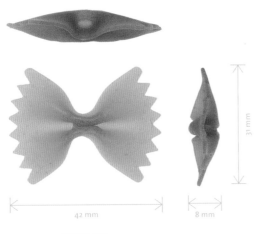

42 mm   8 mm

31 mm

FARFALLE

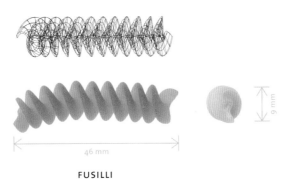

46 mm   9 mm

FUSILLI

Tubular Pop

Ziti and penne are created by means of extrusion and both feature a hollow core and a smooth surface. Penne, among Italy's favorite pastas, is a popular base for both thick and more liquid sauces – while the smooth surface does not absorb too much sauce, the hollow core can be completely filled. Ziti are among the toughest pastas to eat, though, even for Italians, as they are too large to be rolled easily around the fork, especially when the sauce makes them slippery.

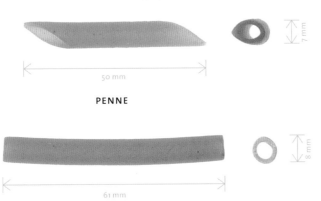

50 mm   7 mm

PENNE

61 mm   8 mm

ZITI

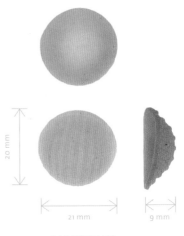

20 mm

21 mm   9 mm

ORECCHIETTE

Arts & Crafts

Orecchiette (little ears) and strozzapreti (priest stranglers) are more traditional, craft-based types of pasta. To this day, they are often handmade and their irregularity is a gift to the palate. Orecchiette comes from the region of Puglia and is traditionally served with broccoli rabe and generously laced with garlic, olive oil and chili peppers. Strozzapreti, living up to its name, comes from the traditionally anticlerical region, Bologna. Both orecchiette and strozzapreti are suitable for chunky, meat-based sauces.

92 mm

8 mm

STROZZAPRETI

Spaghetti Modern

The three famous types of long pastas, whose names are variations on the same theme ("little ropes") show subtle but telling differences. While spaghetti and pappardelle are made of plain semolina dough, fettuccine is made by adding eggs to the mixture – in the typical tradition of the Emilia-Romagna region – and is curled to dry in nests after being cut from a sheet of dough. While the traditional accompaniments are meat sauces for fettuccine and pappardelle and tomato sauce for spaghetti, this pasta is extremely flexible and can be prepared with almost any sauce.

6 mm

FETTUCCINE

1 mm

SPAGHETTI

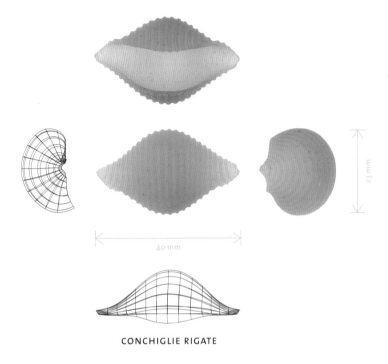

40 mm

23 mm

CONCHIGLIE RIGATE

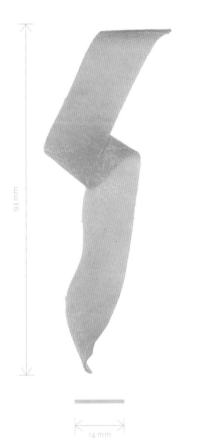

93 mm

14 mm

PAPPARDELLE

260 mm

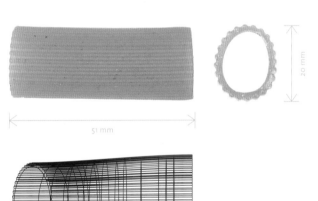

51 mm

20 mm

RIGATONI

Structuralism

Both conchiglie (seashells) and rigatoni (large grooved tubes) present a richly ribbed outer surface and a hollow core to retain chunky sauces. Rigatoni is an extruded pasta par excellence, while conchiglie requires a further step – curling – to assume its final shape. Bigger conchiglie, in the southern tradition, can be stuffed with chunky and heavy meat-based sauces and cooked in the oven.

From top to bottom: Naan, bagels and focaccia – bread, like pasta, is an example of a basic foodstuff that takes on different shapes and form according to functional, cultural and symbolic considerations. Bagels, for example, originated in Poland, but became popular throughout Europe as a means of commemorating the heroism of the Polish in helping to defeat the Ottoman army at the siege of Vienna in 1683.

naturally come together in national groupings. And its chefs are taking inspiration from their national culture to produce gastronomic value which can be easily exported all over the world. Dialect seems the path to a truly universal language.

The commodification of national identities in a homogenized world is boosted and supported by the national governments themselves. Each country seems to have its own manual of style, a listing of positive stereotypes built to reinforce and expand the country's international market. 'Made in Italy' and 'Made in France', even in cuisine, are two examples of labels that contain a whole set of cultural references for the use and consumption of buyers all over the world. When nationalism coincides with material culture and with spontaneous production to address real local needs, brand new products and foods are invented which can become international standards. Fax machines, for example, were developed by the Japanese to overcome the difficulty of printing and transmitting messages in kanji characters from and to parts of the world other than Japan. Likewise, fast-food hamburgers have been added by many rich countries to the range of available choices. In some other cases, local culture is identified with handmade craft production, a simplistic view that does not have much bearing on the global technological market.

The fourth chapter of *Megatrends 2000* (1990), the futurologist bestseller by John Naisbitt and Patricia Aburdene, was devoted to 'Global Lifestyles and Cultural Nationalism'. Although the book, featuring a vast array of predictions about the future of society, is today considered by some to be obsolete, it presented some innovative observations that still carry a strong echo. The delicate balance between national pride and the appeal of a global lifestyle was examined in the book with the help of such diversified case studies as IKEA, McDonald's and fusion cuisine, Benetton advertising campaigns, ETA and IRA, Québecois dialect and Catalan language. Global telecommunications have indeed been responsible for an apparent homogenization of the world, as well as for many ugly mutant neologisms, such as Starbucks, moccaccino (cappuccino with chocolate) and frappuccino (cold shaken coffee with milk), but at the same time they have sparked a lively renaissance of local popular and material culture.

Although this evolution can be noticed in almost all aspects of human interaction, it has been particularly lively in the world of architecture, design and gastronomy. Architecture and design, just like the preparation of gastronomy, are two of the most ancient and spontaneous human activities. For this reason, they are efficient examples for many anthropological and socio-economical studies. Throughout the course of the century, the three disciplines have actively participated in the progressive globalization and re-definition of visual and material culture. In the process, they have provided some of the most engaging and advanced examples of how local and global culture can interact and enhance each other.

This text is expanded from an article originally published in I.D. magazine's (New York) special issue on food published in September 1998.

Right: Nobu, New York, a fashionable Japanese restaurant specializes in 'fusion cuisine' – mixtures of flavours from different cultures. Recently tasted at Nobu: a Japanese tuna *sashimi* combined with medallion of *risotto alla milanese*.

Chapter three

A British feast

Photographer Martin Parr
takes a look through the lens
at the British way with food.

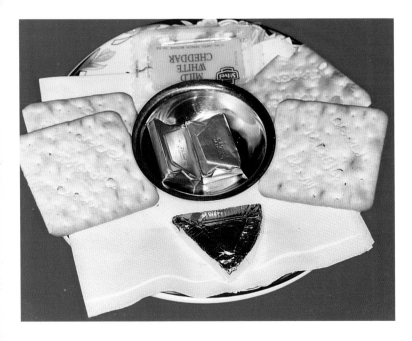

Chapter four

Future food

Joanna Blythman

Designer food: until quite recently, those words would have seemed a contradiction in terms. For almost two millennia, the food we ate had changed very little. Food was food, a product of the primordial earth, of man's gritty toil, of natural forces beyond our control.

Over the past 50 years, technology has moved into food production in a major way. It had to happen sooner or later. Already, we can buy eggs whose nutritional composition has been altered with the goal of preventing heart disease, and scientists are working away developing other miracle 'nutraceutical' or 'intelligent' foods: everything from an 'improved' broccoli that might combat cancer to a potato that protects against hepatitis B.

Some 60 per cent of processed food is now genetically engineered. In the past, when scientists wanted to 'improve' food, they were able to breed within the same species – wheat with wheat or cattle with cattle for example. Now they can identify the gene responsible for a desired characteristic, copy it, and insert it into another species. They can swap genetic material between two different species – such as a tomato and a fish – a huge genetic change that could never occur naturally. So, for example, scientists have now transferred an 'anti-freeze' gene from a flounder into tomatoes, strawberries and potatoes in the hope of making them resistant to frost. Courtesy of biotechnology, that lunchtime sandwich, that baby cereal, that chicken tikka ready meal – all of these could already contain a genetically engineered ingredient. There are thousands more of these altered foods on trial in scientific laboratories and in field experiments around the globe, waiting for the official go-ahead. In the future, genetic engineering could literally reshape what we eat using this mix and match approach. In the next millennium our food could be constructed from the genes of hundreds of unrelated species of animals, insects, bacteria and plants.

Above: Factory workers grade tiger prawns under ice in Bangadeniya, Sri Lanka. It is easier to buy south-east Asian tiger prawns in most Western supermarkets than local produce.

Below: McDonald's serves 13,000 customers a minute and has 15,200 restaurants in 79 countries worldwide.

The food we eat is changing the way we approach it too. People used to cook. Now increasingly we buy ready meals to reheat, made possible by the recently developed 'cook-chill' process which enables food to be cooked at high temperatures and then chilled rapidly. Thanks to an elaborate technological 'cold chain' and an infrastructure dependent on road transport that supports it, cook-chill food can be shipped out from a central factory to supermarket depots all over the country. Once home, we are told we can store it for days in the refrigerator or months in the freezer then reheat it in the microwave when needed.

That microwave, of course, has changed radically the way we eat. No more sitting around the family table for a communal meal, we live in the age of 'staggered eating', when everyone just helps themselves to what they feel like, when they feel like it. We are too busy doing other things – such as watching a constant stream of celebrity chefs on television – to find the time to cook.

Modern consumers have an unprecedented selection of foods from which to choose. Huge supermarkets with acres of parking in out-of-town shopping malls offer us year-round availability of seasonal produce.

Their centralized style of doing business makes it impossible for them to buy a six week crop of strawberries from the grower 30 miles down the road yet they find it feasible to fly mangetout from Kenya to Heathrow and then onwards to our shelves in less than a day. The concept of changing seasons is increasingly redundant, and local produce seems less available as technology opens up our global larder. The shopper in Preston or Glasgow now finds it easier to buy south-east Asian tiger prawns and reconstituted Japanese crab sticks than Morecombe bay shrimps or West Highland langoustines.

Foreign travel has opened our culinary horizons, taking us to exotic destinations to discover exciting new dishes. But it seems that almost everywhere we go, from old world heritage cities to new, relatively undeveloped holiday destinations, we also discover yet another set of golden arches and the inevitable cola culture. At home or at work, whether we eat out or in, big corporations increasingly offer us the same formula techno-food wherever we are from Beijing to Bratislava.

In fact, the current pace of food change is so rapid that now, on the threshold of the new millennium, the question has become how far will technology alter the face of food production before other forces that mould our culture reign it in? Will we be content to move into an age where the natural processes which have produced food since time began are viewed merely as a set of building blocks which can be altered by technology to meet what we are told are our changing needs and desires? Do we really trust an approach that thinks it can improve on nature? Can the world's diverse regional food cultures survive in the face of one global techno-food culture, driven by powerful transnational corporations?

However much a technological approach to food seems currently in the ascendancy, it is clear that many consumers are against it. As fast as fields of experimental genetically engineered crops have been planted in Europe, groups of saboteurs have arrived to dig them up. These groups consist not of an extreme anarchist fringe, but of many ordinary people who believe

First Choice ready meals –
complete meals for
expeditions to extreme
environments. Over the
past 50 years both food
technology and changing
social and cultural needs
– including foreign travel
and expeditions – have
led to the development of
new food products.

Opposite: Genetically engineered tomato coloured blue to highlight its difference. The tomato was the first genetically engineered food on the market in the form of the flavr savr, 1994; which was specifically designed to stay firm and avoid spoilage during storage and transportation.

Above: Battery hens. Farm animals, previously free-ranging, are now kept in crowded conditions indoors, fed pellets and regular doses of antibiotics. Intensive production methods such as these mean animals are prone to diseases that contaminate foodstuffs.

that genetic engineering is taking arrogant risks with our food chain and the environment. Although in the US, the public seems to have rolled over for the gene food revolution, Europe remains intransigent. Poll after poll shows that over two-thirds of consumers do not want to buy and are suspicious of genetically engineered food. So great is that resistance, that Monsanto, the US company spearheading the introduction of genetically engineered foods to the European market embarked on a huge advertising campaign to sell the 'benefits' to a doubting public.

Bullish attempts to convert consumers to biotechnology and its questionable advantages have produced a noticeable anti-food technology backlash, reinforcing a critique of modern food production that started after the Second World War, when technology began to shape significantly the food we eat with the use of man-made chemicals. At the time, the promise was not designer food but a world free from food shortages, where miracle fertilizers would massively increase production and pesticides would deal with the pests and illnesses that had limited output in the past.

As with the gene food revolution now, change happened quickly. Land use altered visibly around the world. Traditionally, farming has been labour-intensive and a biologically diverse range of crops was sown in the traditional rotation that had been the sustainable modus operandi for centuries. Then farmers were encouraged by governments and chemical companies to cut back on laborious husbandry and plant a much reduced number of hybrid strains of crop over vast areas of monoculture, grown with the aid of chemical fertilizers and pesticides.

Keeping pace with the changes on the arable front, farm animals, previously free-ranging and natural feeding, were progressively moved indoors, into factory farms where compound feed pellets and a regular dose of antibiotics could dramatically shorten the time they took to grow to maturity, upping production by previously unthinkable margins.

But even within 15 years, a certain cynicism about technology's vaunted 'benefits' was creeping in. Rachel Carson wrote *Silent Spring* – her landmark critique of the impact of agricultural technology on the face of the countryside – in 1962. By the late 1970s, it was becoming apparent that the Third World 'Green Revolution' predicated on hybrid crops and pesticides that was going to feed the world's starving people, had failed to deliver its much-trumpeted promises. Meanwhile, Europe's unusable food surpluses in the form of grain mountains and milk lakes were becoming increasingly embarrassing to proponents of new, 'efficient' agriculture.

Previous pages: A worker tending lettuce seedlings in a hydroponic culture greenhouse. Hydroponics is the cultivation of plants without soil. Here, the roots of the plant are immersed in a trough through which nutrient-rich water trickles. Hydroponics was first proposed in the 1860s, but reached commercial scales in the 1930s, particularly in the US.

Opposite, above and right: The Chorleywood Breadmaking Process (CBP) reduced the production time of making a loaf of bread, but led to dissatisfaction from some consumers.

Already in the late 1980s, the ongoing agricultural disaster in Britain known popularly as 'Mad Cow Disease' (BSE) was seeping into the public consciousness. By 1996, the government admitted that there were human deaths through eating beef, beef produced according to government advice by animals fed on growth-boosting concentrates – the technological designer replacement for the natural fodder crops that had sustained them for centuries. The BSE episode marked a huge watershed in the way consumers think about food. In Britain, public confidence in the wholesomeness and safety of the food supply dropped to an all-time low. People began to question the idea that food progress equals food technology, which is something of a departure from the past. Ever since the Industrial Revolution, people have been impressed by technology. Why should its application to food be any different?

The classic example of the people's love affair with food technology is breadmaking. No sooner had industry technologists devised what is now known as the 'No-time' or 'Chorleywood Breadmaking Process' (CBP) back in 1961, than British bread became uniform and relatively unsatisfying. But the CBP also allowed bakers to work with a reduced workforce, bypass the traditional slow fermentation stage and turn out a cooled, sliced and wrapped loaf in a record three-and-a-half hours from start to finish. The Chorleywood process was technologically clever but in commonsense terms, stupid. Britain became infamous for its processed bread but it took over from craft bread nevertheless. Wrapped and sliced CBP bread now accounts for 80 per cent of the bread the Nation eats.

Of course, small, old-style craft bakers cannot compete with the cheap, industrial product. They went to the wall. Connoisseurs who remember what good bread is all about have been left complaining that bread doesn't taste like it used to. They fantasize about 'real' bread made to time-honoured methods such as the rustic boule that is produced from the legendary wood-fired ovens of that revered baker – Poilane – in Paris, whose archaic production methods and inspiring taste have given his product a cult following. A handful of new-wave bakers have sprung up to cater for the disaffected bread lover and to revive artisan skill.

Since their business is one of scale and bulk, large food retailers cannot respond to this on-going criticism of modern technological breadmaking techniques. They have tried to address it, not by sourcing locally or seeking out craft products, but en masse with a better, 'improved' technological solution in the form of 'Bake-off'. This is mass-produced industrial bread that is made in one central national bakery then dispatched frozen to be baked in supermarkets up and down the land, presented in traditional shapes and with all the fresh feel-good factors attached to the real McCoy.

In France, traditional French bakers have even taken to the streets, forcing the government to prevent those the craft trade refer to as 'reheaters of bread' from passing their product off as 'le vrai'. In Britain the lines between real bread and techno-bread have long since been so blurred, that Bake-off has been welcomed with open arms by consumers as an improvement on the dreaded 'wrapped and sliced' loaf.

It is not just the British who are taken in by the allure of new food technology. Since the 1950s, even peasanty, relatively non-industrialized

Following pages: Food is no longer just a product of the farm and the kitchen. Additives, artificial flavourings and new production techniques have changed some food into evermore fanciful – and unrecognizable – forms.

parts of Europe have been enthralled by the endless stream of novelties that technology can produce. Food was no longer just a product of the farm and the kitchen, but of the scientific laboratory. Developing an armoury of modern additives, scientists got to work on changing the food we eat into evermore fanciful forms. But by the 1980s, when consumers were beginning to wake up to the effects of some of the first rudimentary chemical colours and flavours that gave us candy floss and prawn cocktail flavour crisps, the industry had moved on to what was presented as the relatively enlightened world of 'natural' colourings and 'nature-identical' flavourings.

Like children at Christmas, food technology keeps us wondering what the next novelty will be. Early discoveries included instant coffee, developed for American troops during the Second World War and cheese spreads: cheese broken down into its constituent parts and then assembled with lots of additives.

Nowadays, the look of a processed food is as, or even more important than its contents. The straightforward old yogurt pot, for example, is out. Many yogurts now come in rigid two-compartment plastic containers with a dinky addition to mix in. Anything goes from multicoloured sprinkles to chocolate drops and mini-biscuits – with the caveat that it must be sweet.

Everything can be miniaturized from processed ham and cheese with salty crackers to self-service, pick and mix miniaturized cheeses. The fish fingers that ousted fresh fish fillets are already out of date. Now the processed article frequently comes in a fishy shape, just as poultry comes in dinosaur-shaped kievs. For some sophisticated adult consumers, expensive processed food is packaged in an upmarket presentation box, bearing the approval of a celebrity chef. One technological gimmick is followed by another. What's next, we wonder?

Gimmicky presentations are frivolous, but they could become a virtual substitute for real food diversity. The large corporations that invest in our food chain and want to control it are beginning to look like the Indiana Joneses of the food world, raiding our natural food heritage and making it their own. A Texas-based plant breeding company has recently obtained a patent in the US which allows it to call strains of rice it has developed 'basmati' even though they will be grown outside India. For some 20 years, the same company has been selling a 'Texmati' rice in the US, described on packets as 'US' basmati rice. More recently, it added 'Jasmati' rice to its portfolio, which it promotes as the 'Texas-grown copy of Jasmine rice from Thailand'. Its new patented rice is sold in the US as 'Kasmati' – a play on 'kashmiri' and 'basmati'. Predictably, this move has infuriated the Indian government which says the patent could severely damage its considerable basmati export market and put producers of the authentic item out of business. Environmentalists say that the concept of patenting was created for original industrial inventions and technology, such as the telephone, but that it is quite wrong to apply that principle to plants and animals because that downgrades the status of life forms to 'inventions' which can be owned by powerful commercial interests.

Basmati rice is one of the first foods to attract the interest of northern hemisphere 'bio-prospectors', seeking out what is now being called the 'green-gold' of natural biological resources by first laying claim to them and then extracting royalties from farmers who wish to use them.

With patenting in the air, countries south of the equator which hold the bulk of the world's biological resources or 'germplasm' are having to find ways to keep that in common ownership. India, for example, has no law to protect names like basmati and the patent on it has increased demands for the country's bio-wealth to be catalogued before it is appropriated by companies aiming for monopolies over other important food crops.

While large corporations work at a global level to make food production into an artefact that they own and control, our educators are reinforcing the technological message. Frequently, British children no longer learn to cook at school, a situation made more acute by the fact that unlike their European counterparts, few stand much chance of learning to do so at home. Historically, our industrialized workforce was quick to make the transition away from home cooking to manufactured processed food. Our dislocation from food production happened early, spawning generations who think a gravy is only made with granules and a custard only from a packet or tin.

At school now, this process is legitimated. The old-fashioned Home Economics has been replaced by food technology. Educationalists, recognizing the way our food chain is being altered by technology, now think it is more important that children learn to design an industrial process for manufacturing fish fingers than to learn to cook fish. It is sad that people no longer cook very often, alas that's the modern world. Children need relevant skills, we are told.

It is not just in schools that technology in food is in favour. It is also widely presented as offering a solution to intractable problems – everything from food shortages to chronic illnesses. But as steadily as profit-driven corporate technology finds applications in food, it also

Opposite: Onion omelette
sponsored by Fuji. Above:
Potato omelette
sponsored by Calvin
Klein. Both designed by
Martí Guixé. The ultimate
goal with sponsored food
is for it to be offered as a
free meal.

becomes clear that it creates new problems. It is a familiar plot line. Technology offers a solution. The solution works partially but also causes problems. Technology then comes up with a new and 'better' techno-fix to solve the problems it created and so the cycle continues. Thus, when it becomes clear that eating processed junk food can make people fat, the processed food industry doesn't want consumers to stop eating its products and turn to healthier unprocessed fruit and vegetables; it wants people to eat its new 'lo cal', 'lite' and 'diet' processed junk food instead.

The technological treadmill is particularly marked in meat production. The factory farming of animals that came into vogue during the last 50 years has thrown up problems for both animal welfare and human health. Kept intensively in unnatural circumstances, animals are prone to a range of diseases, now widely referred to as 'diseases of intensification'. Various official surveys have revealed, for example, that between a third and a half of all chicken eaten in the UK is contaminated at point of sale with campylobacter and salmonella: two dangerous bacteria. Reported cases of food poisoning in the UK went up by 600 per cent between 1985 and 1995 and intensive meat production methods are heavily implicated in this staggering rise.

In Sweden, where consumers are more suspicious of technology and traditionalists hold sway, this problem has been addressed by a back-to-basics approach, banning the use of preventative antibiotics on animals and encouraging more sustainable and humane production methods. In Britain, public opposition in the late 1980s killed off the idea of adopting the American 'solution' of irradiating meat. (It was not clear whether this technology did 'clean up' the meat anyway and it seemed to reduce its nutritional value.) Rather than focus on why livestock-rearing methods produce contaminated meat in the first place, the food industry prefers to deflect the reponsibility for food poisoning on to the consumer.

In the US, a new wave of 'anti-bacterial' products has been developed – everything from chopping boards to hand cloths and sponges – impregnated with chemicals to kill all known germs. Now British supermarkets are promoting these and using them in their own food handling in the endless battle against food-borne pathogenic bacteria. Meanwhile, scientific journals lead on research which suggests that these anti-bacterials may actually create a new generation of resistant 'super-bugs', potentially more harmful than those they say they can defeat.

It is clear that the application of technology to the food we eat has already resulted in many spectacular failures and shortcomings. Despite this, there is a feeling that technology nevertheless represents unstoppable progress and that one day it will all come good. This idea is fostered by the large chemical and biotechnology corporations that are investing heavily in the food chain. They dismiss objections from those who say that new food technologies are non-scientific and irrelevant, and neither useful nor desirable.

Here, a case in point is the genetically engineered growth hormone, rBST. This hormone, when injected into a cow's udder, can make her produce up to 40 per cent more milk. But in Europe, where milk production exceeds demand, it has been the subject of a moratorium until January 2000. Opponents say rBST will lead to increased intensification in milk production, and link it with adverse health effects in cows and even a possible increase in certain kinds of cancer in humans. Some farmers fear it will be the product that does for milk what BSE did for beef.

However, the pressure is on from the financial interests that have invested in developing rBST to see that this product is allowed into the European market in the new millennium. As the example of genetically engineered foods shows, many consumers feel that even if they do not want such technologically altered products, they will get them anyway.

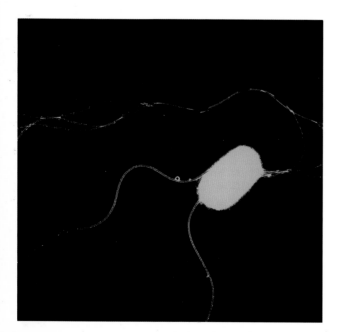

Left: Salmonella enteritidis. False colour transmission electron micrograph of the bacterium. Various official surveys have revealed that between a third and a half of all chicken eaten in the UK is contaminated with campylobacter and salmonella.

Opposite: Coloured transmission electron micrograph of Escherichia coli (negative stain). E. coli occur normally in the gut flora of humans and warm-blooded animals. Virulent strains of E. coli such as o157 are associated with food poisoning.

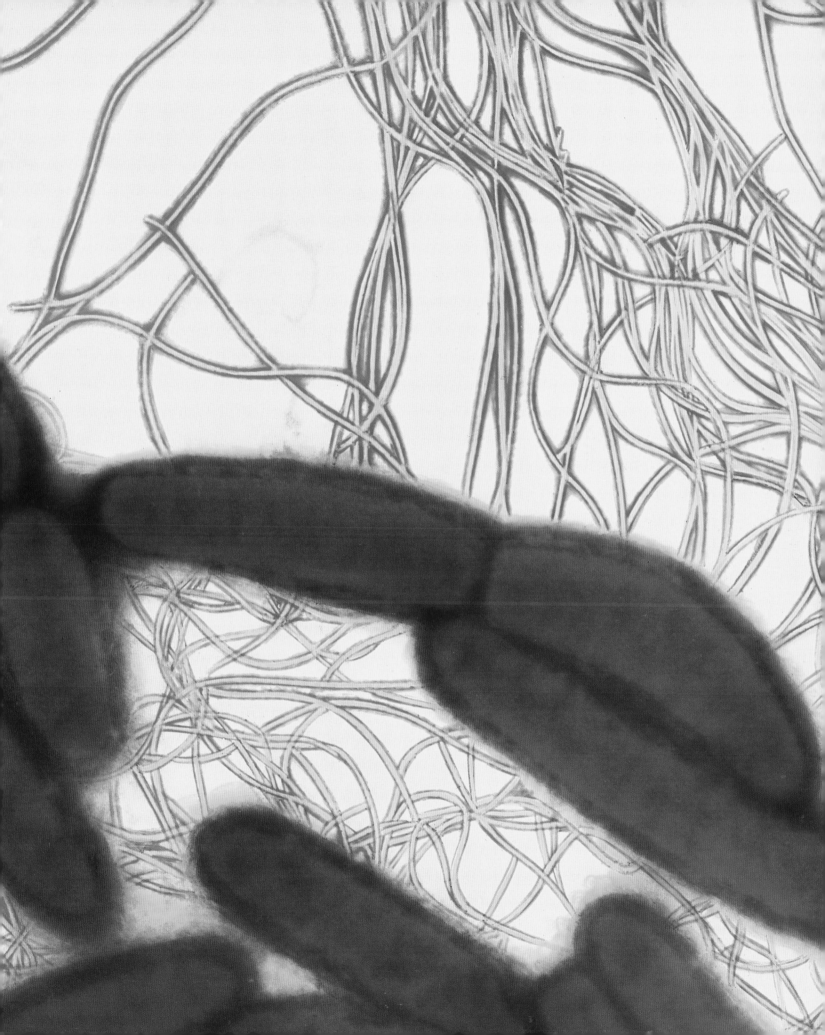

Few governments or legislators want to be seen as blocking the path of scientific progress and turning the clock back. As more consumers become progressively alienated from the technological drift in modern food production, organic food is on a major roll throughout Europe. Consumers increasingly see it as a 'safe house' in a world where unbridled technology is compromising the safety and integrity of what we eat.

In Germany, more than 95 per cent of all baby food sold is now organic. In Britain, large food retailers that in the past blew hot and cold over organic food have had a second coming and are now jockeying to have the biggest and best organic profile. Though concern for the environment may in part drive this change of attitude, it is clear that retailers are keen to associate themselves with organic produce because consumers find that reassuring – a natural antidote to technological tinkering with food.

Even in the US, home of the large corporations that develop much of the food we eat, organic food is emerging as the strong contender to counter techno-food. In California, there are now chains of supermarkets, selling only organic food and throughout the US, farmers' markets selling locally grown organic food are becoming common, offering a qualitatively different shopping experience from the uniform selection at the shopping mall.

Once beleaguered traditional food is reasserting itself. Vegetable box schemes offering a direct producer-consumer link have taken off. In Europe, where many shoppers already felt happier with their calico or cane shopping bag than the supermarket trolley, traditional food markets, focusing on regional specialities are going from strength to strength.

In Italy, a body called the 'Slow Food Movement' has been set up to counteract the drift towards global techno-food. It is promoting the symbolic concept of a Noah's ark for food to protect traditional foods that are being systematically squeezed out of production by a deluge of standardization and worldwide distribution. The European Commission has devised special certificates of status to protect traditional foods.

All this is part of an ongoing struggle over the kind of food we want to eat. The traditionalists' vision of a food ark is a celebration of diversity in food, of regional specialities which reflect local cultures and which work with nature. The technologists' future food vision is a uniform one with global applicability. They see a food world where all the diverse populations of the globe are united by the same formula products – be they foods, or processes for producing food – owned and controlled by huge transnational companies. We will have to wait and see which force will decisively shape our food for the future.

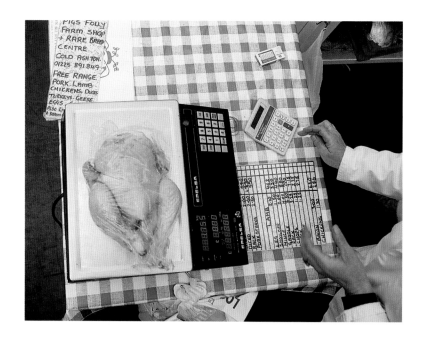

Above: Corn-fed free-range chicken on a scale at Bath Farmers Market. Left: Organix Organic Breadsticks for babies. As more consumers become increasingly uncomfortable with technological developments in food production, so they have turned towards organic food for reassurance.

This page: Merricks Farm organic fresh produce box. *You* Magazine (the *Mail on Sunday* supplement) runs an annual award in conjunction with the Soil Association. Merricks Farm were finalists in 1997 in the organic box scheme awards.

Following pages: Toys from McDonald's. Multinational fast food corporations offer enticements to keep children coming back for more.

Chapter five

The lure of the aisles

Jonathan Glancey

Left: The term 'Super
Market' was developed
in the 1930s in the US to
describe a new method
of selling, based on the
concept of 'pile it high,
sell it cheap' and self-
service. This Alabama
grocery store of 1910,
although well stocked,
still employed service so
it was a precursor of the
supermarket. Above:
Alabama grocery store
(1926).

Supermarkets smother the globe. They are the places most people go, mostly by car, to stock up fridges and freezers, often with far more food than they need or want for the week ahead. The market is dominated by a few major companies which are household names. These are big businesses for which food is a commodity like any other. They rely heavily on packaging, marketing, advertising, customer loyalty schemes and corporate identities to buy and maintain their share of the market. They make mind-boggling profits.

Supermarket buildings are almost without exception big (almost by definition), brash and dominant. They are often ugly, although many have ambitions to be taken seriously as architecture. They gobble up vast amounts of land in city centres, and even more on the edge-of-town and in the heart of the countryside. They feature large car parks. They sell a bizarre range of foodstuffs sourced worldwide. These require the expenditure of prodigious amounts of energy to get from A (as in Accra, Acapulco or Addis Adaba) to B (as in Birmingham, Bradford or Bangor). The overwhelming desire the British supermarket shopper appears to have for prickly pears, kumquats, alfalfa, mangosteens and ugli fruit, let alone blackcurrants in March, Cox's Orange Pippins in June or strawberries in December is all but incomprehensible to overseas visitors who shop for food in seasonal markets. Supermarkets have put thousands of small businesses – butchers, bakers, greengrocers – out of business. For better or worse they have changed the face of the high street. They know neither time nor season. They are open early and late seven days a week. Unlike God they do not rest, even though they can well afford to do so.

So much for the positive side of supermarkets. What of the strange forces that drive them? Why do people find them so compelling? Why do we shop for food as if servicing a car? Why do we prefer the neat environment of supermarkets to the sensual atmosphere of street markets and small, specialist shops? The answers are complex and no one essay can get near to anything like a full answer as to why people are drawn to these peculiar air-conditioned, fluorescent-lit food processing machines like moths to a flame. Yet, our love affair with the supermarket nurtured over half a century is a phenomenon that richly deserves analysis.

Let's start with a seemingly odd question. Why eat the out-of-season kumquat? What possesses us to want to spend a disproportionate amount of our incomes on exotic fruit that has very little taste and precious little nutritional value after its long voyage from southern China? In its native Guandong province, the little kumquat is quite delicious. Amongst the food prepared for Chinese New Year celebrations are gleaming bowls of kumquats: they represent gold or money and are proffered as a symbol of financial luck in the year ahead. The kumquat shipped to supermarkets from China has little taste and no meaning. Why buy it? Especially why buy it in preference to locally grown, cheaper and tastier seasonal apples? For one thing delicious apples are increasingly hard to find. Many supermarket-bought apples taste strangely of blotting paper. They are quite good for us, but not much fun to eat. The kumquat on the other hand is exotic. We buy it perhaps as we do much exotic supermarket food because it is decorative. Kumquats and the tongue-twisting litany of

"Look–Mother! This register figures our change!"

3.97

New *National* Cash Register stops mistakes in figuring change!

THE NATIONAL CASH REGISTER COMPANY, DAYTON 9, OHIO

"Land sakes, this IS a nicer way to buy lettuce"

Here's why smart shoppers prefer fruits and vegetables in Cellophane

DU PONT
Cellophane
DU PONT

BETTER THINGS FOR BETTER LIVING ... THROUGH CHEMISTRY

John Rose the King's Gardener presenting Charles II with the First Pineapple Grown in England, at Dorney Court, attributed to Hendrick Danckerts, c.1670, engraving. Exotic new fruit and vegetables first came into Europe from the US in the sixteenth and seventeenth centuries. Just as today we regard tropical produce as sophisticated, so these early plants became highly prized.

curious and largely tasteless fruits that fill the modern cornucopia that is the supermarket shelf exist to decorate our tables, much as fashionable restaurants in the 1980s served virtually anything and everything from sirloin steak to sea-bass ringed with cranberries from the US, kiwi fruit from New Zealand and other fruity gewgaws designed to titillate our eyes, but not our taste buds.

Buying (and selling) exotic fruit and vegetables is, by extension of this argument, a sophisticated activity. It says, perhaps, that we do not eat to live but live to eat decoratively. Thus we dine today, thanks to the supermarket, as only kings and queens did when the first pineapple arrived in Britain in the late seventeenth century.

The corollary of this argument is, of course, that the taste and quality of these globe-trotting fruit and vegetables are unimportant. What matters is their decorative value and the fact that they show that we live in the sort of decent, egalitarian society in which a taxi driver may share a kumquat with a king. We are all sophisticates now. The old school greengrocer condemned us to eat boring old apples and pears, peas and potatoes and, then, expected us to go appleless in the spring. Today, thanks to the supermarket we can eat whatever we want whenever we want like so many spoilt children and all

this in air-conditioned, squeaky clean comfort. No waiting in high street rain. No potatoes to wash and scrape. Cleanliness and comfort are two further keys that help to unlock the mystery of the supermarket, which strips the beastliness from meat, the soil from spinach. It sweeps away the detritus of street markets. Its appearance is nearly as clinical as an operating theatre. No shopper would ever guess that the pork chops on display in the chilled cabinets of the 'meat' section were ever a part of a mud-loving piglet. No one need ever know that vegetables grow in fields, that cheese is best when made in what supermarkets consider unsanitary conditions which is why the consumer is forced to find a specialist supplier.

Our squeamishness means that we do not want to know about the processes by which our food arrives on spotless supermarket shelves. The supermarket absconds us as shoppers from all responsibility. In them we are innocents. We do not have to think of the implications – emotional, moral, ecological or economic – of cheap food presented as if impeccable in Tesco, Safeway or Sainsbury's. The supermarket means never having to recognize that meat is the produce of a once living animal. Many people find the sight of whole slaughtered animals or live animals destined for the pot on display in traditional markets abhorrent. Or the sight of unpackaged

or unrefrigerated food worrying. They find it difficult to come to terms with the idea that food is food, not furniture or home decor, and that good, delicious food must be fresh and often prepared, and even killed, on the same day as it is eaten. The heady sensuality, the brutal and sometimes sudden carnage of traditional markets, especially those in the land where kumquats are grown, are so far removed from the contemporary British experience of shopping for food, that it is these older ways of life that seem somehow unnatural. In other words, the British are separated almost entirely from the reality of traditional and natural food production.

This line of thought leads us out from its well-stocked, hygienic shelves to the design of the supermarket building itself. Supermarkets are bizarre structures, hovering awkwardly between town hall, market building, car showroom, exhibition hall and the concourse of modern airports and railway stations. In essence they are, and need not be more than, giant sheds, uniformly lit and planned around the optimum volume of trolley-pushers who can be processed through them from fruit and vegetable counters to check-out via booze and sweets as quickly as possible. This though has never been enough. Supermarkets are part of an intensely competitive and usuriously profitable industry. Competitive advantage is made and hopefully sustained not particularly by the quality of the food on offer (this is, by and large, a given except at the very top end of the market) but by price and image. There is a tricky equation to be balanced here. The supermarket can either go for the low design input-low price option (on the pile 'em high, sell 'em cheap principle) or invest in design and push the prices higher. Both calculations are made and practiced by supermarket chains.

In Europe and elsewhere in the world, traditional markets are patronized by people of all incomes and no matter how cultured or educated. Good, fresh, delicious food bought daily, prepared, cooked and eaten with love and care is a great leveller. Except in Britain where the supermarket has replaced the market. Translated into architectural terms, these class divisions in Britain have seen the chains adopting different design strategies. Sainsbury's has commissioned well-known architects to style the facades of its stores both in and out of town. The results are curious. Thoughtfully detailed High-Tech, Po-Mo, Pseudo-Classical and Neo-Modern screens are erected in front of big sheds to give the appearance of great sophistication. Shop here, these wanton facades seem to say and you are the sort of person who buys the *River Café Cook Book*

Consumer preferences are determined by their beliefs and attitudes. Grouping customers by their beliefs is very difficult, but retailers have found one way of gathering the relevant information. Reward cards allow the major retailers to analyse in great detail what their customers are buying. Although it does not give total accuracy as far as consumption is concerned, it does help them to procure, promote and stock the products which their customers require.

There has been a 41 per cent decline in the number of grocery retailing outlets in the UK from 62,222 in 1979 to 36,931 in 1987. The number of superstores in Britain has risen from 239 in 1980 to 1125 in 1998. Just six companies control 51.9 per cent of the total grocery market.

In 1995 there were 4,596 new food product launches. Many of these are not on the shelves today, having failed to meet consumers' needs; some will have been successful for a time, after which subsequent new products will have superseded them. Few will last longer than five years without having to be adapted or updated in some way.

Continent supermarket, France. By far the most significant change in food retailing in the 1990s is the importance of the consumer and consumer preferences. This has meant a huge expansion of choice, quality and service, and the development of the ethnic food market, exotic foods, own label and convenience foods.

(One and Two), goes to art exhibitions and buys the best extra-virgin oil. In other words, these architectural cosmetics are designed to affirm, and re-affirm every weekend, a sense of middle-classness.

Tesco and Safeway have largely gone for the village-barn, old-town-hall look. This folksy style writ on a gigantic scale is partly a response to local planning constraints (even if out of scale with their surroundings and rather ugly, they fit the planner's idea of Britishness, of the vernacular idyll, and can be found the length and breadth of the country skinned in a uniform garish brick no matter whether the traditional local building material is primarily stone, flint, yellow brick, red brick or clapboard). They are also a representation of Middle England (or Middle Wales and Scotland) values. They are meant to be somehow traditional, homely and polenta-free. They are designed to appeal to people with fitted kitchens who like ready-prepared meals except for a traditional 'roast' (shrink-wrapped beef, shrink-wrapped lamb) of a Sunday, although as Sunday is simply another shopping day it is hard to know quite why the roast still has its special place on that day.

At the bottom end of the social spectrum come Gateway, the Co-op and others which appear to make no concessions to styling. In this sense they

are less tortured and more honest than their middle-class contemporaries. What you see is what you get, simple tin-box buildings piled high with cheaper cuts of meat and fewer exotic vegetables.

In Europe and the rest of the world, these design distinctions between supermarket chains barely exist, if at all. This is because the supermarket, where it exists, performs a different role. Shopping for food is still largely undertaken, enjoyably, in city centre shops and city and village markets. Household goods and bulk foodstuffs (rice, flour, oil) are bought from the equivalent of supermarkets. These are very often no more than industrial sheds beside arterial roads. They do not need the level of design that Sainsbury's, for example, invests in its shops because bulk foodstuffs do not need anything like the same kind or degree of marketing input that it takes to convince a middle-class British shopper to buy exotic or fashionable food.

For the fit and employed, the supermarket is seen as a model of convenience. As shopping is a chore, then at least it can be done in one fell swoop on the weekend and by car in some comfort. The supermarket run may well have its frustrations – waiting for a parking space, queueing at the till, the family row on the way home – but at least it saves having to bother with lots of old-fashioned shops.

As the British are so passive when it comes to buying food (or eating it in second-rate restaurants) they can be sold most of what they feel they want in plastic cartons that are designed to flatter the food they guard, but, more importantly, to be easy to stack and transport. The fact that people are prepared to buy food without knowing how it smells is quite astonishing. One of the greatest pleasures of food is its appeal to our senses of taste and smell. For the supermarkets, the fact that we are embarrassed by 'smell' ('uh, it smells', say the British, rather than 'ohh la la' when first encountering a ripe camembert) is a gift that even their battalions of accountants are hard-pressed to value highly enough. Supermarket shopping although superficially about choice – so many different brands of tea, coffee, mineral water, factory eggs, barn eggs, free-range eggs, organic eggs – is actually supported by our passivity. We do not exercise our freedom even to choose between one cut of meat, one cheese or another. We buy food from supermarkets in exactly the same way as we do washing powder and disposable nappies. If once we had the power to choose, we have lost it somewhere in the brightly lit aisle of the supermarket.

This passiveness that, in part, has caused us to lose our power of choice goes deeper still. We say that we are concerned about the environment. We check to see whether a particular brand of shampoo has been tested on animals. We are proud that our hairspray as well as our well-stocked fridge is 'CFC-free'. We drive to the local 'recycling mini-station' and put brown glass (Belgian beer!) in one giant wheelie bin, green glass (Rioja Reserva!) in another. Oh, what clear consciences we have as we fill up the car with unleaded from the petrol station at Tesco and Sainsbury's. And we try to eat a balanced diet, just the right amount of roughage, green vegetables, olive oil and oily fish (and some red wine too!). And yet we accept the fact that so much of the food lining the supermarket shelves has been picked in dismal conditions by desperately poor people in what we like to call 'developing countries'. Choose to ignore the fact that the food we cannot even be bothered to smell before we buy, the shrink-wrapped or prettily packaged food we heave into the trolley for all the world as if it was a plastic football, has been driven again across the world, and that this great adventure has been hugely costly in terms of the use of fossils fuels.

And then we have the cheek to believe, without ever expressing this, that the convenience of supermarkets outweighs the absurd number of road journeys needed to stock them, by vast intra-cooled, turbo-charged lorries, and the gallons of petrol we burn in driving to and from them to buy food we often take no real pleasure in either buying, preparing or serving. This ecological rumination is just the tip of a polemical iceberg. We say, for example, that we love the countryside and going for Sunday walks through it. We also want supermarkets, which is why we are prepared to raze great tracts of land we say we love to build these places of passivity.

The only consolation for anyone who questions supermarkets and the superglue-like grip they have on British shopping and eating, is the fact that their star may well be waning. Slowly, ever so slowly, yet the rising interest in home deliveries, shopping by e-mail or the internet, and the tiny tide of people who have made the choice to return to living in city centres ... these things have punctured a small hole in the vast, flatulent bubble that is British supermarket culture. These, though, are early days; in any case it is far more important that the British, perhaps with the rising influence of Europe (particularly France, Spain and Italy with all their wicked, sensual Latin ways) begin to learn to like food and thus to treat it and the way it is grown, nurtured, cut, butchered, spiced, transported and sold seriously. Whilst we insist on treating food as a chore and leave the selling of it to those who are more interested in money than manna, the supermarket will keep us passively in its insatiable thrall in which design matters more than the food itself.

Top: Target supermarket, Phoenix, Arizona, US.
Above: Auchan hypermarket, Le Havre, Normandy, France.
Left: Asda supermarket, Corby Shopping Centre, Britain. In Europe, shopping for food is still largely undertaken in city centre markets. Supermarkets perform a different role to those in Britain and the US – providing household goods and bulk foodstuffs.

Following pages: Japanese UK shopping centre Yaohan Plaza. Staff start the day with slogans.

Picnic, Mougins, 1937.
L–r: Nusch and Paul
Eluard, Roland Penrose,
Man Ray, Ady Fidelin.
Photograph by Lee
Miller. The picnic –
nature, companionship,
a good bottle of wine –
it does not take a 'self-
consciously' designer
environment to create
the perfect ambience
for a meal.

Chapter six

An angel at my table

Will Alsop

The table is often but not always the supporter of food. This horizontal plane can influence the ambience of the meal. Too big, too low, too wobbly, etc. and it destroys even the very best food. Even an ugly table, dressed in the right way can transform a mere morsel into a feast. In Italy, one's immediate surroundings are transcended by the appearance of the table. Even in the middle of some 1950s industrial estate, tables can be seen covered with a check table cloth, protected from the sun by a rogue vine, simply laid with two white plates, two glasses, two knives, two forks, a bottle of wine and a simple pesto. Two friends sharing a meal talk of their home towns and their mothers. In their eyes the ugly surroundings do not exist. Food, combined with a carefully prepared table, offers a simple pleasure which is the essence of conviviality.

Living in London, I am particularly aware of the renaissance in eating out and a general improvement in food quality as a result. I am convinced it is now possible to eat better in London and consume a wider range of cuisines than in any other city in the world. This availability of food brings with it a certain trap of fashion, however. Not only do we have designer restaurants, we also have designed food. It started with nouvelle cuisine, which artfully covered larger and larger plates with less and less food. This has now evolved into what I call the 'heap', which is served on a succession of beds of food and presented on very large, slightly dished white plates so that the juices can be contained. 'Art' gravy is now de rigueur.

I would question the whole idea of design and its importance in eating. At best the design should not be obvious. The whole point of design should

Right: Jean-Paul Sartre and Simone de Beauvoir at La Coupole, Boulevard du Montparnasse, one of the Paris cafés that became the regular haunt of a generation of philosophers, artists and like-minded people. They used cafés as places to meet, work, eat and drink, often spending the entire day and evening there.

be to give maximum comfort to the diner, whether they are alone or in a large party. The designer restaurant all too often threatens discretion and dignity with a tyranny of coolness. Compare the relative comforts of a transport café with the close-packed discomfort of a typical designer restaurant. A good transport café allows space around the tables with attentive but largely invisible waiters. The fashion-conscious restaurant charges high prices for the privilege of being treated like a moron. A knowledge of the names and the tastes of edible and (inedible) leaves is necessary before you enter the door. The transport café specializes in well-prepared familiar fare and, apart from its location, its success is dependent on not letting the customer down with a variable menu. A well fried rasher of bacon is a precarious art form, consumed by a very discerning public.

My distrust of the obviously designed is in part born out of recalling a variety of memorable meals, and the realization that very few of them have been consumed in one of the current rash of fashionable restaurants. This does not mean to say they have not been designed, or that they don't depend on the quality of the food, but they all depend on the table and its placement for the creation of delight. Sometimes history itself creates the ambience. None of the examples I will give has anything at all to do with

the evolution of rudeness, which has developed as we have progressed from etiquette to cool, or anything to do with the idea of food as uniform.

The first recorded meal is the eating of the apple in the Garden of Eden. From this single exploration of the delights of the forbidden came the *raison d'être* for all the eating establishments of the future. Places were established to tempt the senses into indulgences of passion and lust, by and large resulting in pure unadulterated joy. The nearest meal I recall to the Garden of Eden was actually on the banks of the river Eden in New South Wales, Australia. The river Eden rises somewhere in the Blue Mountains and drops off the plateau, which is Australia, on to the coastal plain where it manages to wind itself slowly to the ocean. In the area of its very last existence as a river before fresh water gives way to salt, in the brackish areas of the organism, the forest of gumtrees with its floor of wild Aaron lilies, it becomes breathtakingly beautiful.

Having risen from my bed in a tin hut I wandered into the village bakery and purchased a loaf of very crusty white bread. The bottleshop surprised me by stocking a New Zealand wine and even more so by it being Cloudy Bay. At around lunchtime I walked along the banks of the Eden armed with my victuals and a stout knife, until I found some oyster beds. My meal was

Opposite: The classic British fry-up – prepared in time-honoured tradition by the transport café and unsurpassed by any designer restaurant.

This and previous pages: A good transport café is a perfect example of an environment in tune with the needs of its customers: comfortable, homely surroundings, serving familiar foods from an unvaried menu with the minimum of fuss.

simple and delicious, accompanied by kangaroos drinking the river water and koalas in the gumtrees. My sketch book offered a recreation, beyond the sheer joy of being there. The experience of being alone in beautiful surroundings with all the accoutrements of sensory pleasure generates a rich memory which will feed your imagination from time to time until you die. This raw material of memory becomes a fertile field for embellishment, which allows a pleasant memory to become a myth. Myths set the standards for one's future comparisons. This standard was high. Simplicity, quality, tranquillity are all ingredients to suit my particular mood on occasion. Can you design these elements or do they lie beyond the brief for a designer? Is the 'designed' situation only ever an approximation of a series of natural phenomena?

The innocence of the Australian picnic, new bread in a new country, can be contrasted with a winter lunch on a grey day on the banks of the river Elbe just to the south of Hamburg. Hamburg is a city looking out to the world because of its port; it stands with its back to the Fatherland. In 1988, I left Hamburg and travelled south. By lunch-time I was hungry and decided to stop at a down-at-heel edifice. The building, with its deeply pitched roofs and peeling cream paint, did not exhibit the international stylistic optimism of Hamburg. This building was nineteenth-century German; the day was damp, dull and dismal and the interior contained the day very well. The huge ceramic wood-burning stove in the corner failed to warm the inner man. The empty dining room offered me the best place to sit, between the stove for warmth and the window for melancholic views over the river. Lunch arrived on the wooden table. A large plate with very heavy stainless steel cutlery and a plastic container for the mustard. The food was traditional sailor food called 'Knipp'. Heavy and delicious, it consists of brains and other offal of which it is perhaps better to remain ignorant. This is comfort food; easily eaten with a fork and served with English mustard, it manages to warm the interior of the body and slowly revive the spirits of a homesick sailor with a stodge that is easily prepared in a ship's galley. I sat there contemplating the possibility that not only the hotel but also the menu had not changed in 50 years. After lunch I decided to return to Hamburg for fear of venturing too far into Germany.

Typically the accoutrements that support a meal have emerged through convenience. Knives and forks save getting the hands dirty, or indeed contaminating the food with the dirt on the hands. Nearly all cultures in our global, shrunken world have adopted the same aids to eating. This can give rise to odd facts; for example, I do not understand why in Thailand, whose indigenous population is rather small, the people seem to use the heaviest cutlery, while Americans, who tend to be large, often use minute eating utensils. The placement of tableware has gathered around it an etiquette, which is often used by the upper classes as a means of recognizing the lower classes. It used to be that anyone holding their knife as though it was a pen was automatically understood as being both ignorant and uncouth. These things do change, often by inverted snobbery. The Heinz Tomato Ketchup bottle is now perfectly acceptable as an object to be placed on the table, although a bottle of Daddies Sauce is not. In former times, bought sauces were either never used, or decanted into

Traditional German café fare: sausage, rye bread, mustard and a glass of beer – perhaps the equivalent of the British bacon and eggs with a mug of tea.

HERR ST.

R.K. Stanleys restaurant in London specializes in Bangers 'n' Mash – designed to emulate the British transport café and traditional luncheonette, right down to the bottle of ketchup and stainless steel salt and pepper shakers.

I have already discussed picnics but I do find them, weather permitting, one of the most satisfying forms of eating. You choose your own restaurant knowing that the menu is perfect for you because you have taken it with you. When I observe others choosing their spot I often wonder why they sit in one place as opposed to another. (I observed one couple laying a picnic on the roof of a multi-storey car park.) However, there are a series of eating establishments which I suppose should be called restaurants but which I prefer to call 'picnic plus sites'. Just outside Marseilles at the end of the *calanques* at Sormiou (near Cassis) is such a spot called, rather unpromisingly, Le Lunch. It is only open during the summer months and is little more than a concrete platform in the sea with a kitchen on it. The descent down to the establishment, which takes you through a succession of hairpin bends, is terrifying and surpassed only by the ascent which might be a few bottles of Bandol Rouge later. At night this permanent picnic spot (I advise dinner as opposed to lunch) is illuminated by the moon reflecting on the limestone cliffs that surround this fjord-like inlet. The ambience is extraordinary as it combines with the tempo of the waves lapping on to the small beach. The food is simple and direct. It consists of a variety (not too many) of fish dishes plus one meat dish, which is always lamb chops. The potatoes are always prepared in the same way, while other vegetables are non-existent. I call this a 'picnic plus site' because the place is fixed and the menu is known before arrival. There are no surprises, only the delight of certainty. All the design effort that exists in the place went in choosing the spot. Its simplicity is a true celebration of this part of the world.

A similar picnic plus site was enjoyed by my wife Sheila and I in Turkey in 1976 on a beach in the south where lobsters, ordered the night before, were kept fresh in a hole dug in the beach as they awaited our arrival. This practical use of nature enhanced the meal, giving an air of the special to a very simple menu.

Big menus are not my favourite. I know that a wide choice means that the likelihood of the microwave increases. Moreover the element of too much choice is daunting. Architects often talk about presenting multiple options. I do not subscribe to this activity because I am the person who is being paid to advise on what I think, through my experience, is best for the project and client. This allows an architecture to be truly discovered by both myself and the user. I like the chef to be confident that two or three choices will be delicious. The chef is the professional and I am quite happy to place my judgement in his or her hands. (I have, incidentally, a similar view of hairdressers who ask what you want them to do.) Bruce MacLean and I have often discussed the idea of the 'no choice' bar with only one hot dish on offer each day. If you do not like it, do not come. In America there are places in the mid- West for under 21s (21 is the legal drinking age) called 'No bar/No grill'. This takes the idea of limited choice to a new dimension, where there is no choice at all. Young people rush to them because they are in effect extensions of their own bedrooms. The idea of extensions of the home gives rise to the rather old-fashioned concept of dining rooms. The concept is clearly offered as an alternative to cooking at home. These were popular (in the 1920s and 1930s) in cities like Glasgow and their success

a sauce boat. Some of these habits, or manners, appear to be meaningless, others are important. The size and shape of the glass for different wines is important as it affects the taste of the contents. A big red wine needs more air in it than a light white. Whatever the do's and don'ts of napkins or serviettes, sipping soup away as opposed to towards you, putting butter on the side of the plate and not spreading the bread directly from the butter dish, the freedom of diners to express themselves as they wish is often related to the name of the establishment they are eating in.

Canteens assure a certain speed of eating and noise level which minimizes the requirement for manners. I am still not sure if you are supposed to eat off the tray or lay the table and discard it. Pepper, salt, sauces, butter all come individually wrapped and are all disposable, like the cutlery. There is no difference between the appearance of the tray and the presentation of food in a canteen and economy-class eating on aeroplanes. A canteen is supposed to be quick and cheap; eating on a plane is also quick but should take longer, as it is eating which often whiles away the hours of boredom during a flight. In both these eating establishments, traditional meal extenders are omitted. Cheese, coffee, chocolates and liqueurs are all designed to stretch the duration of a meal which enables conversation to extend into new and often intimate areas. Canteens and planes also prohibit smoking, but a good Havana elevates the occasion of eating to a calming and satisfying state which can give either a deep sleep or a sense of dignity to the table talk, and therefore to ban smoking in these very different eating establishments is unacceptable.

Lufthansa dinner in economy class. Shrimp salad, grilled chicken and rice, cheese plate and hazlenut mousse. The design of the airline meal is perfunctory and denies other important aspects of meal-times – savouring a delicious wine, taking time to digest between courses, basking in good conversation and the company of friends, perhaps enjoying an after-dinner cigar.

Above: Launceston Place, London, established 1986. Opposite: The Reform Club, London, established in 1836, offers the right combination of grandeur and comfort appropriate for large banquets. The building it now occupies was designed by Charles Barry in 1841.

was largely due to the idea of a sense of intimacy, ease and quality at affordable prices. The cost in the UK of eating out in many establishments is extraordinarily expensive, which represents a real threat to eating out as a sustainable experience. Fifty pounds per head is beyond the reach of the majority of people. Added to the mark-up on what is often a modest wine, this verges on the criminal.

Dining rooms should be timber-panelled with large, polished gate-leg tables, a sideboard and chairs with arms. No table cloth is required, just silver salt and pepper pots and a very generous vase of cut flowers. Such dining rooms are currently missing from our choice of eating establishments, but there should be places for dining with friends in this style.

These are the opposite type of room to the Japanese style. Japanese style is often cited as a major reference for minimalism, but I think this is just a convenient underpinning for a style which imposes a particular burden of behaviour on those who are unfortunate enough to have to suffer it. The food in Japan is extremely varied and, in the main, delicious. The attention to detail comes in the way you consume it. First of all you and your companions have your own room, with your own cook, who prepares food at the pace you would like to consume it. Each dish is really a series of morsels which allows you to mix and match as you wish. Because you are sitting cross-legged on the floor, the air of ritual and correctness is very apparent, but in reality there is no real code. A variety of drinks are quaffed, for example: water, sake, tea and whisky are all consumed in no particular order and are topped up throughout the meal. A mouthful of tea is followed by a gulp of whisky. There is no perceived end to the meal, and as cooking utensils (as well as the gas rings) are washed up en route, you can stop anywhere, any time you have had your fill. It is a wall-to-wall experience focused on conversation and eating; there are no set rules and the minimalist surroundings are simply there to keep out the weather, in themselves they are not a statement. The Japanese experience, for me, falls into the category of 'picnic plus'.

Banqueting rooms occupy the other end of the spectrum. They are best used as a means of celebration. By definition they should be grand and focused on a single large table. A banquet requires at least 25 people. Fewer than this and it is reduced to being a feast. In London the banqueting suites in many of the large hotels have completely lost their style by succumbing to an idea of flexibility (apart from the traditional establishments such as the Reform Club). They are in fact multi-purpose halls that can adapt themselves to the needs of conferences or an exhibition tennis match. They are always let down by those horrible aluminium-framed stackable chairs (usually anodized in gold) which are both unconvertible and ugly. It is no wonder that hotels continue to be the worst designed semi-public buildings in existence. Their owners seem to despise architects, often on the grounds that they 'know' what their customers want. They clearly do not. I helped consume a banquet at the Hôtel de Ville in Bordeaux. The room was magnificent and managed to firmly establish a sense of occasion without really trying. The large and highly polished table was laid with individual place settings which not only included all the cutlery you

needed but also your own salt and pepper, array of glasses, menu in a holder, napkin ring, etc. In other words each place was a complete table for one diner. The chairs all had arms and were suitably upholstered to give maximum comfort. Proust said that the most important thing about theatre design was that the chair should be so comfortable that the sitter becomes unaware of their own body. Banquets have the same requirement.

The meal consisted of a large number of courses, each of which was accompanied by a particular wine. Being Bordeaux, every bottle was delicious. Towards the end of the meal a small chocolate delight was served, which is apparently a delicacy unique to the mayor of Bordeaux. The recipe is a secret that has been handed down from chef to chef. The idea of a single dish that can be obtained at only one table in the world is an extremely powerful concept, and in itself has the power to nail the meal firmly to the vagaries of your memory. Imagine if every table you ever sat at could offer you a complete novelty – it would change your idea of geography.

Novel to me, but not presumably to the Mexicans, was the choice of three starters at a restaurant in Mexico City. They were worms, ants or grasshopper. When offered this you immediately look around to other tables to try to obtain some glimpse of what any of these dishes might be like. Having arrived late I was devastated to find that everyone else was well into their main courses and puddings. I opted for the grasshopper, which turned out to be similar in texture to very small prawns but more delicious. The contents of a meal can obviously strike fear as well as anticipation in the unsuspecting diner.

The Grand Opera Café (which used to be called the Café Budapest) in Moscow, which is not a café but a cabaret, offers yet another style. This huge restaurant used to be one of Lenin's favourites, and certainly while sitting in it, it is difficult to escape the knowledge that one of the fathers of communism used to eat and drink there. The knowledge of history is as powerful an ingredient as the chocolate delight in Bordeaux. It makes the experience special. In Vienna, at a restaurant called Oswald and Kelp, they serve goose on Martini day to celebrate the way in which the goose saved them from the Turkish invasion by raising the alarm. It is of course strange to offer thanks to the goose by eating it.

In the Grand Opera Café the guests arrive and leave their own coats, hung properly, in the cloakroom. I have always liked the idea of one's excess baggage being taken away in a professional manner. The neo-classical interior is bedecked with a series of long tables all properly dressed with white linen table cloths and fine cutlery (David Mellor would be jealous). The waiters are suitably attired in dinner jackets and all is apparently set for a dignified evening. Once you are seated, the gentility of the occasion falls away as, unasked, a bottle of vodka and a glass is presented to each person on the table. You have to ask for wine, which they do have, and eventually a fine bottle of Georgian wine arrives. While you are waiting, a succession of courses arrive for your consumption, all of which are revolting. Thank God for the vodka. Whilst you are grappling with the food, something else happens. Slowly a stage automatically emerges and a show starts: dancers, jugglers, singers, contortionists, knife-throwers, etc. It is a

very old-fashioned style of entertainment, but hugely enjoyable, as to my Western experience it is unique. The show ends as the food stops coming and the stage slides back, but the band remains. By this time the one thousand diners are drunk and happy. They begin to rise and dance until everyone is on the floor, dancing with anyone from beautiful Russian girls to not so beautiful female truck drivers. The band plays on and the vodka keeps coming until a whistle blows and everyone and everything stops. Everyone retrieves their coats and steps out into the cold with big smiles on their faces. A good time has been had by all. The experience is extraordinary because everyone has been subjected to a piece of designed time. The original design of the premises was intended to add a sense of grandeur to lunch but this was all made incidental to the pace of the evening. It was the clearest demonstration, to me, of the dimension of time being properly considered. Time is so badly considered, if at all, by London restaurants.

Pub grub, cafés, bistros, tapas, meals-on-wheels, Sunday lunch (washing up to 'Round the Horn'), eating on ships, planes, etc. all offer their own specific ambience for the consumption of comestibles. Some have a fixed location and others are mobile (that is, boats and picnics), but all of them should be wonderful experiences all the time. Our experience tells us that this is not always the case. The ingredients for success, in my opinion, are simplicity, uniqueness and dignity.

I see an evolution at some point in the future where the world becomes a huge table, a plane of consumption where it is possible to eat anything, at any time, and every spot is celebrated with beauty. We already have the availability of 'all day breakfast', why not 'all day everything' which truly reflects the emerging freedom from the conventional timing of the day? Perhaps breakfast, elevenses, lunch, tea, high tea, dinner, supper and night cap will become words belonging to a past view of life, which simply leaves us with one word, MEAL.

For me the design of the restaurant is secondary to the food. The only truly important design elements are the table and the chair combined with the service.

Above: *The Cook, the Thief, His Wife and Her Lover* (directed by Peter Greenaway, 1989). A film which explores the odd connections between sex, eating, love and death. A wealthy gangster visits a fashionable restaurant while his wife conducts a passionate affair with a fellow diner. Below: *Babette's Feast (Babettes Gaestebud*, directed by Gabriel Axel, 1987). Lottery prize money is used to prepare a sumptuous banquet. Below right: *Eat Drink Man Woman (Yinshi Nan Nu*, directed by Ang Lee, 1994). Exploring how families use meals and food preparation to appease their hunger for love in stressful times.

Travel notes on kitchens

Ettore Sottsass

When I am invited to dinner by my friends or to elegant houses or even to restaurants, as soon as I can, when and if I can, I go and see what the kitchen is like. I don't go and look at the kitchen for the sake of gossip or to conjure up rather funny or rather sad visions: I go to see kitchens because I picture them like the sort of corridors and places you find behind the stage in a theatre, where the performance is calmly, fearfully or (sometimes) cheerfully prepared, or maybe with conceit and with suspense – the performance that always has to be marvellous, the performance that always has to enact some slice of life, perhaps the whole of life; the performance with its lovely lights and fine words, its beautiful songs and handsome gestures, with its strange music that floats on the distant, abstract and dusty air of that empty cube, the stage.

I see the kitchen as that faintly mysterious place, where in actual fact the ingredients are prepared for a kind of sacred performance, a ritual repeated daily and connected with the continuation and at the same time the consumption of existence, concerning the continuous rebirth of existence and at the same time the constant confirmation of its precariousness and provisionalness.

I mean sitting down for a meal at table, or starting to eat, I mean 'being able to eat', even sitting on the floor, even on a train-station bench, even sitting in a car on the highway, with the food handed through the window, even in the craziest situations, it is always something of a miracle, always brief or a long event that involves us and our stories and the stories of the people around us, all abandoned to our solitary frailty and to our frailty on this planet, abandoned in the midst of other animals, in the sky, on the earth and underwater, in the midst of grass, leaves, funguses, lichen and moss, surrounded by hardnesses and softnesses, surrounded by meats, intestines, mucus, jellies, blood, salt, sugar, drugs, tastes, odours, perfumes, acidities … I always think the kitchen is the place where this infinite encyclopedia of substances and planetary states is collected and gathered and put together, organized, catalogued and proportioned; where it takes shape, takes on some sort of recognizable sense, and is transformed into something that can then be used to design that ritual, the daily ritual of eating.

So as soon as I can I go and look at the kitchen to see what's happening,

Above: Milan, Italy, 1991.
Opposite: Navaka, Fiji,
1978.

to discover the secret of the performance that's going to be given; I do it
as one goes to see the painter in his studio, reads his biography and
scrutinizes his drawings and his notes, to wrest the secret of his art.

One always tries – if possible – to watch out of the corner of one's eye –
those corners where life, where events, start getting inexplicable, and also
to understand where and how people decide the enclosures of sacrality, the
ones with which they always attempt somehow to stem the unbearable
invasion of mystery ...

Around those steaming plates and sacrificed meats, around those fat,
drugged sauces, those small glasses always full of wine, there were days
when existential awareness, a romantic patriotism, and the metaphysical
experience of the uncertain earth, of woods and waters, rains and snow, of
hidden mushrooms and cyclamen in the shade; there were days when
suffocated lust, the threat of wars past and wars to come, the forecasting of
marriages, of children to be born, the sign of the ages that transformed
hands, hair, the way of turning around, and even the way of looking at
women and children – when all this and other things besides, rose to such a
pitch in the general emotion that neither silence, nor words were any

longer enough. Songs would begin to fill the kitchen, songs sung without a smile, sung with eyes gazing into space, chasing the normal stories of everyday life, stories of betrayals, loves, illness and heroism …

My Uncle Camillo's kitchen, deep in the shadows of the Alps, was a well-proportioned stage for a big general performance of life; as were the older kitchens that I have seen, with a black saucepan hanging from the centre of the ceiling all blackened by soot and with a hole in the top, so that the fumes and vapours and tastes of existence would not lose contact with the high sky inhabited by mystery and would perhaps also let the high protecting mystery down into the dark vault of the kitchen-room-house.

Then, very slowly, perhaps on account of socialism that seemed to have found a system of 'rationalizing everything', even the way of cooking polenta, or perhaps, as the capitalists say, 'owing to the excessive cost of land', or maybe because in general there was the 'machine civilization', the civilization of industry and important things like these – I don't know – one fine day they invented the idea of a 'minimum existenz', with the smallest apartment in the world, the smallest kitchen in the world, all calculated to the length of a person's arm and the number of steps to be taken to fill a saucepan with water, to turn the gas knob and switch on the gas, to boil the water, get out the can of dried vegetables, open the can, put the dried vegetables into (previously salted) water, wait X minutes as written on the can, pour out the soup, carry it to the table (as near as possible), eat, go back with plates and glasses, put them in the dishwasher, turn knobs, listen to the humming of the boiling water, take them out and put them back in the closet.

The smallest kitchen in the world is so small that you can really stand still in the middle of the room and cook at great speed and without effort, kind of very, very fast food, heated up at home, or for example, a 'very fast TV-dinner', such fast food that you hardly actually see the stuff at all and in any case you won't see it because in the meantime you're watching television.

The idea that 'food must not be seen, that you musn't see what you eat', must be an idea thought of by those ultra-puritan people (who are everywhere in the world), I don't know, but I do know that those people, if they had been able to, or if they could eliminate any pleasure, any lewd gluttonous enjoyment, any juicy, happy, bright event in life, would have done so or would do so immediately …

Deposited in the world's smallest factory, all clean and spruce, all white with fine plastic laminate doors that allow nothing to be seen, with all the machinery set out in orderly rows, nicely enamelled and attractively chromed, are the supplies, with all the raw materials, or rather the semi-cooked and the ready-mixed, the frozen foods, the dried foods, tidily stacked, all deposited in rational order, with all the cans, all the large and small cardboard boxes, the bottles, the jars and the airless packages, the plastic plates, the plastic glasses, the packets and the mineral water, the milk carton, the neatly arranged meats, the squashed pieces of bled white chicken, the well-sliced and well-washed vegetables, the peas all alike, the fillet of sole already fried, the mussels already soup and then also the

Above: Filicudi, Italy, 1983. Below: Zhaoqing, China, 1995.

mustards, the mayonnaises, the foie gras, the soft cheeses with their tinfoil, the cheeses in wood, the vinegars, the oils, the butters, the powdered spices, the beans in water, the semi-cooked corn-on-the-cob, the artichokes without the spikes ... everything is fine and ready, there's no problem of leftovers, nothing to be touched, only cans to be opened or bottles to be shaken, powders to be emptied; nothing is ever touched with the hands, so it's all very hygienic and there aren't even any odours because the drops of perfumed odorous fats have been frozen, washed away, everything in short, even the food has been washed away. Eventually what's left are the numerous boxes large and small, the cans and jars, bottles and flacons, all with their shiny labels, their layers of packaging and tinfoil, their cardboard and paper, the tissue paper and cellophane and, finally, the glosses with the colour photographs of what's inside, beautiful photographs, with the right lights, the sunlight of a winter's dawn, lights that even let you see the dewdrops on plums, peaches and grapes, and other special lights that illustrate the reddest meat, the greenest cabbages, the fattest olives and the shiniest beans, intact.

The packs, boxes and cans are delightful things: like Swiss cigarette and chocolate stores. The print is laid out by 'graphic designers' who know all there is to know about print, and the colours of the illustrations are outstanding, sometimes even phosphorescent. Sometimes the illustrations are printed in Singapore on immense rotary presses at amazing speeds, all polished and perfect. In the world's smallest kitchen, as if it were the world's smallest supermarket, everything is in its proper place, in

137

compliance with carefully thought-out codes ... without anyone getting tired, without anyone going off on any long journeys, without anyone having to do anything difficult, in fact nothing difficult at all.

Into the world's smallest kitchen has crept a very beautiful, fantastic world, where neither poverty nor anxiety nor errors nor sickness nor deformations, nor confusion exist, where lettuces have not even one rotten leaf on them, where cherries have no worms in them, where oranges are all the same, fine round and shiny outside and in, where you don't find one orange all blood-red inside and all the others a wishy-washy yellow, where the lemons don't have black marks on them, where the artichokes leave nothing to be thrown away, where everything is bigger, juicier, sweeter, better proportioned, happier, better-looking, brighter-coloured, as on a television screen, like the girls in *Vogue* who never have toothache, who never have been jilted, like dreams in springtime, like that fanciful fantastic garden of Eden, more or less painted by Rousseau 'le Douanier', where the tigers sit as good as gold to have their photograph taken and the green mamba dangles from the tree and makes eyes at you. In the world's smallest kitchen by now the new rituals unwind by underhand methods, beyond the deafening din and the suffocating air of life.

The new rituals slip over the photographs on the labels, glide quickly over the gloss on the paper, over the dewdrops, censuring unhappiness, censuring doubt, censuring uncertainty. And so the world will always be a beautiful place and everybody happy. All the time we will travel through a slow, permanent rain of lovely labels, such heavy, thick rain that through all those labels we won't even be able to see what there is, perhaps, on the other side; or what may possibly be on the other side. We won't even want to see, because we'll be perfectly happy with what there is on this side ...

Only on Sundays does the barbecue take over. On the lawn in front of the house, as on an organized journey into the forest, we can see real smoke and smell the real smell of beefsteak, of real meat burning. Usually it's the man, the husband, the fiancé or the lover who acts so boldly, putting on an apron and picking up the real meat, the beef. The ancient kitchens, the ancient rituals, are memories that sometimes come back on Sundays. The scene is the front lawn that sends out a reasonably fresh perfume, surrounded by small trees and shrubs that are more like ornaments than vegetation, with a friendly dog also wandering around, more of an ornament than a 'household pet', maybe with the blue swimming pool nearby, more like canned water than a lake.

The new rituals have more or less these types of stage: the orange-coloured chairs of the fast foods and the stackable chairs of the self-services, the distant kitchens, stainless steel landscapes, the highway canteens between one gas station and the next, the home kitchenettes, the peasant-style kitchens in solid wood, the big cowboy kitchens with pots and pans hanging on the wall, the memory-store kitchens, the kitchens ...

Reproduced by kind permission of Ettore Sottsass. From an article originally entitled *Travel Notes. Ettore Sottsass on Kitchens*, published in *Terrazzo*, spring 1992, no. 7.

Above and right: Bali, Indonesia, 1978.

Photographic Credits

Introduction
Research Photos/FPG (8/9)
Hulton Getty (10)
The Advertising Archive (11)
Photograph by Jim Sillavan (12, 13)
John Webster/Rex Features (14, 15)
Davies + Starr (16–19)
John Greim/Science Photo Library (20)
AKG (22)
Jim Oliver/Peter Arnold Inc./Science Photo Library (24 left)
I.D. Magazine/Photograph by Graham Macindoe (24 right)
© BBC (25)
Courtesy Zanussi (26, 27)
Photograph by Anthony Oliver (28/9)
Photograph by Mike Duisterhof (31 bottom left)
Focus on Food, RSA (32 bottom)
Photograph by Anthony Denney/Courtesy of the Estate of Elizabeth David (33)

Chapter one
Courtesy of the Estate of Elizabeth David (34/5)
The Anthony Blake Photo Library: © Gerrit Buntrock (36 top left, middle); © Milk Marque (36 bottom); © Maximilian (36 right)
Courtesy Philippe Garner (37 left)
Habitat (37 right)
The Anthony Blake Photo Library/© Victor Watts (38)
Tropix Photographic Library (39 top and middle)
Topham Picture Point (39 bottom)
© BBC (42)
Topham Picture Point (43)
The Anthony Blake Photo Library (44, both illustrations)
Anthony Blake (45)
© Chris Gascoigne/View (46/7, 48)
Conran restaurants (49)
Gideon Mendel/Network (51 top)
Jonathan Olley/Network (51 bottom)
Domus/Donato di Bello (52, 53)
© Chris Gascoigne/View (55)

Chapter two
I.D. Magazine/Photograph by Mikako Koyama (54 left, 55)
I.D. Magazine/Renderings by J. J. Gifford/Funny Garbage (54 middle and right)
Hulton Getty (56 top, 57)
The Kobal Collection (58 left)
I.D. Magazine/Renderings by J. J. Gifford/Funny Garbage (60, 61)
The Anthony Blake Photo Library: © Milk Marque (62 top); © Eleanor Bell (62 middle); © Tim Hill (62 bottom); © Jane Stockman (63 top); © Gerrit Buntrock (63 middle)
© Steven Freeman (63 bottom)

Chapter three
All photographs © Martin Parr/Magnum Photos

Chapter four
Rosenfeld Images Ltd/Science Photo Library (78/9)
Tropix/© M. & V. Birley (80 top)
Sipa Press/Rex Features (80 bottom)
Anthony Oliver (81)
BSIP Estiot/Science Photo Library (82)
Peter Menzel/Science Photo Library (83)
Blair Seitz/ Science Photo Library (84/5)
John Ross (86, 87)
Anthony Oliver (88, 89)
Designed by Martí Guixé; photograph by Inga Knölke (90, 91)
P. Hawin, PHLS, University of Southampton/Science Photo Library (92)
Dr Kari Lounatmaa/Science Photo Library (93)
© John Carey/The Times, London (94 top)
Anthony Oliver (94 bottom)
The Organic Picture Library (95)
Anthony Oliver (96/7)

Chapter five
Corbis (98/9)
Corbis/Bettmann/UPI (99 right)
The Advertising Archive (100, both illustrations)
The Bridgeman Art Library/Private Collection (101)
© Chris Steele-Perkins/Magnum Photos (102/3)
The Anthony Blake Photo Library: © Graham Kirk (104 top and right); © John Sims (104 bottom left)
Homer Sykes/Network (105)
Paul Reas/Network (106 left, 109 bottom)
© Martin Parr/Magnum Photos (106/7, 108, 109 top)
Paul Reas/Network (109 bottom)
Alex Bartel/Arcaid (110)
Justin Leighton/Network (111 top)
Jeremy Green/Network (111 middle)
Homer Sykes/Network (111 bottom)
Mike Goldwater/Network (112/13)

Chapter six
Photograph by Lee Miller/© Lee Miller Archives (114)
Guy Le Querrec/Magnum Photos (115)
© Dave Young (116/17, 118, 119)
Robert F. Hammerstiel (120/21)
Phil Starling (122)
I.D. Magazine/Photograph by Graham Macindoe (123)
Photograph by Sasha Gusov/Launceston Place Restaurant (124)
Elizabeth Whiting and Associates (125)
Kobal Collection (126/7, 129)

Chapter seven
Photographs reproduced by kind permission of Ettore Sottsass/Terrazzo

Photographs originally published in I.D. Magazine's (New York) special issue on food published in September 1998: Davies + Starr (16–19); photographs by Graham Macindoe (24 right, 123); photographs by Mikako Koyama (54 left, 55); renderings by J. J. Gifford/Funny Garbage (54 middle and right, 60, 61).

Index